Ebony Books

Presents

David Simon's

How to Unlock Your Child's Genius

Published by

Ebony Books
PO Box 11627
London SE9 1ZE

© David Simon 2004

First Published 2004 • Second Reprint 2004 • Third Reprint 2005 • Fourth Reprint 2007

ISBN 0 9529355 5 4

Contents

Foreword

The Soul of the Child

Autumn always announces a new school year; a magical time for the great opportunity to learn, and to discover the wonderful world of books. Autumn, in particular September, should have been my favourite month but, this magical reality would be split between the immigrant stories my parents planted in me, and the hopelessness of the school remedial teacher who seemed to summon me each Thursday, as if I was to be caned for my inability to learn. I have never got over this brand of underachievement. Never exorcised the shame of being taken out of the class to make the lonely walk down the school corridor to her makeshift class where, according to the taunts of other pupils, the dumb children went. But I knew, because of the magic of the Caribbean stories that my parents lifted my soul with, that one day, I was destined to be a writer; that one day I would learn, that I would read books, and perhaps even write them. Yes, autumn is a great month, but it can also be the cruelest; offering false hope; banishing the innocence of childhood to the horrid Victorian architecture where minds, like mine, were damaged. For me, like thousands of children in schools around the world, September became the start of winter tears.

Then, like now, this underachievement was never explained. I knew deep down that my soul wanted some other form of education. Couldn't education be an adventure? Couldn't the great quest for learning be met in the school? I was fortunate; my parents gave me the fantasy of achievement. They gave me characters who battled through: like Two-Foot, the man with one leg who lived on their island and became a great mountain climber. They told me about ugly Cousin Jumbie-Toes, who taught himself to write love poetry and ended up marrying the prettiest woman on the island. Although all these stories were untrue, it didn't matter. They simply wanted to plant the seed of miraculous achievement inside of me, knowing full well that, the remedial teacher and the Headteacher, were chiselling away at my dreams.

Unfortunately, for so many other excluded children who weren't fed this fantastic and bizarre oral tradition, their souls died to the wonderful world of learning: the books, the lessons, the teachers, the rules all served to stifle what should have been an adventure. No one tells them what they are being educated for. Abstract reasons are sometimes given: "So you can read and write and get a good job!" The excluded child is likely to come from an excluded parent, who belongs to an excluded family, who belongs to an excluded community. So, in their minds there is no reason for an education. Yet, these children seek the great adventure which life demands.

For seventeen years I have run Ebony Education and seen so many disillusioned and excluded children seek another form of education. The alternative is for the child to seek another education that is relevant to their increasing precarious survival. They might simply be disinterested; never engaging in class learning. Or it might be in a street gang, where, the education of the street offers them status, self-esteem, life skills and resources. This alternative education system has to be monitored by the State. The educational psychiatrist, the educational social worker, youth workers and the police are all part of the army of people that monitor this alternative education. Why? The mythology of rightness, of correctness, of tradition and normality has to be maintained. Child discipline (or some might say punishment) has to be introduced, not so much to correct the child, but to stop any challenge to this mythology. Unfortunately, punishment permeates the education system. Paperwork, irrelevant testing, and poorly designed curriculum all punish the pupil; excluding the culture of the child, excluding the dreams of the child, excluding community genius.

By the end of this ordeal, the child is confused, or scared, or rebellious or a mix of so many emotions. I've noticed in recent years that this state of mind in the child is happening at a younger age. This is not teenage stuff. Children from seven upwards experience this. The education system responds with pseudo-science from all quarters. Reports from various professionals about why the child is doing badly; reports assign blame to the child, the parent, or their peers. The reports, like many of the tests, attempts to project the profession as normal, correct and even caring. Often, it is not.

All these sad events finally leads to the soul of the child running away from learning. Outstretched hands of professionals reach out but they can't catch the child; their spirit is in abandoned flight. But where do they run to? They simply run to their alternative education; an educational system relevant to their survival that offers them self-esteem, status, peer acceptance and economic resources. In truth many flee the classroom for the jail or low paid jobs. The parents and the few who care, don't know who to run to. They seek advice from whomever, and often this advice comes from sources that do not have a true insight into what is happening to their child. The citizens advice bureau, the council official, the well meaning friend or any other individual or group they can think of. It is a hopeless affair.

Over the years over two thousand parents have come to me. I always observe how they sit, how their children behave. Are they agitated, frightened or clumsy.

Now, after seventeen years as an educationalist, I instinctively hear the child's soul. This book is for the parent and all those who care about the child. I started off many years ago catering for the black community, but now parents of all races, have consulted our organisation. The crisis of the child is in all communities. I simply hope that this book will help, you the reader, hear the soul of your child, and those of children all over the world, and join me in helping the child to unlock their genius.

Parents who wish to undertake a formal training course in the Genius programme should log on to our website www.ebonyeducation.com

Introduction

Exploring Genius and the Art of Teaching Your Child

African Proverb
Knowledge is better than wealth:
You have to look after wealth, but
Knowledge looks after you
         Zambia

I have written this book in response to the numerous questions I have been asked over the last seventeen years since I first established Ebony Education. This book is meant as a guide to parents, carers and youth and community workers on how to support the education and life skills education of the child/young person. The purpose of this book is to empower parents, by giving them strategies on how to support their child's education and engage in their development. This book (will enable parents to) aims to:

a) Adopt strategies on how to best educate their child/young person in a culturally diverse society.
b) Provide a holistic approach to education that will empower the parent, child/young person and also the education establishment that the child attends by giving them imaginative strategies in educating the child.
c) Demonstrate how to identify their child's learning style/experience and improve the educational environment of the home.
d) To constructively engage with the school that the child attends.
e) Help devise the child's Individual Learning Plan.

This book provides an educational programme that celebrates culture and education, and is aimed at equipping parents to help realise their child's/ren's full potential. This book is unique in that it recognises that the parent, child/young person and education provider have to collaborate in order to gain the best results. The Genius Method recognises the parents as teachers. This method that I started developing in 1987 consists of:

a) A holistic and creative approach to education.
b) Training for all parents on how to become Parent-Teachers.
c) The creation of a Learning Zone as a positive learning environment for the young learner.
d) The use of integrated assignments to teach study skills, communication skills and life skills.
e) The use of culture as a learning tool and to raise self-esteem, confidence and to develop leaderships skills in the young learner and Parent-Teacher.

The Genius Programme Says:

• The parent-teacher must not abdicate total responsibility for their child's education to any other individual or body.

• The parent must be trained as a parent-teacher.

- The parent-teacher must be part of a team that she/he partly leads.
- The parent-teacher must make a lifestyle change to accommodate this programme which is part of their own and the child's lifelong learning plan.
- This education programme demands that the home be re-designed to create a dynamic learning environment.

Exploring Genius

All children have gifts and talents, the difference between these and so-called genius children was that they had the opportunity to express these talents, which was usually nurtured by parents or a mentor, who gave them the determination, self-confidence, vision and learning environment (home and community) to further develop these talents. This book works on the premiss that all children are potential geniuses and that to access these talents the parent-teacher, or teacher, or mentor has to devise a unique genius programme in which the child can excel. It is also important to remember that for a genius to be recognised, someone else must acclaim them to be a genius. In the case of your child, you must be the first one, and set about developing your child's genius and set about this work with humility.

The Collins dictionary defines genius as 'extraordinary intellectual power'. So let us look at this extraordinary intellectual power which in most children is unrealised. First, from observation we can see that there is a great hidden intelligence working in the human body which is responsible for miraculous things going on which we are totally unaware of: cell activity, digestion, blood circulation, tissue repair etc. We want to be aware of this super intelligence so we can use it consciously. We can start by looking at the Multiple Intelligence Theory which has identified seven intelligences that we can look at:

- Body Kinaesthetic Intelligence, which is concerned with physical movement (exercise, movement, dance and yoga etc).
- Interpersonal Intelligence which is concerned with communication skills, working as part of a group, effective non-verbal communication. Tony Buzan (Brain Child) says that personal intelligence is dependent on the four brain foods: oxygen, nutrition, love and information. We might add a fifth which is peace.
- Intrapersonal Intelligence, which is concerned with thinking about thinking (metacognition), introspection, self-reflection and self-knowledge.
- Logical/Mathematical Intelligence which is concerned with the relationship between numbers, and therefore is about induction and deduction.
- Musical/Rhythmical Intelligence which is concerned with the understanding of rhythm, creative expression, harmony, music and natural sounds.
- Verbal/linguistic intelligence which is concerned with speech, hearing, the understanding of phonemes, words, sentences, humour, poetry and retention and recall.
- Visual/Spatial Intelligence which is concerned with imagery, spatial awareness, recognition of colour, understanding graphic representation and dimensions.
All these lead to peace and spiritual intelligence, which is concerned with the realisation of who you really are. Ultimately this leads you to experience a one

ness with all creation and the wish to serve others. This multiple intelligence model is useful in making the parent-teacher aware of the various intelligences operating in their child.

The Art of Teaching Your Child

Aims:
- To make the parent-teacher aware of the need to create a dual curriculum in order to realise their child's full potential.
- To introduce the parent-teacher to strategies for teaching their child/ren.
- To introduce parents to a holistic education programme.
- To provide parents with the knowledge and skills on how to create a positive learning environment.

What is the Foundation Stage?

The foundation stage officially starts when a child is three years old. The curriculum for the foundation stage sets learning goals. There are six learning areas, which are:

- Personal, social and emotional development.
  Including aspects around behaviour like relationships, confidence and self-esteem, attitudes and self-care.
- Communication, language and literacy.
  Including aspects like language skills, reading and writing skills and thinking skills.
- Mathematical development.
  Including number skills, shape, space and measure.
- Knowledge and understanding of the world.
  Including aspects like exploration, investigation, information and technology, time, cultures and beliefs.
- Physical development.
  Including health, awareness of body, use of relevant equipment and an awareness of space.
- Creative development.
  Including aspects like exploring music, media; the imagination and communicating ideas.

The parent-teacher, seeing the variety and breath of the foundation curriculum, should equip the home with a range of resources to stimulate their child. Here are some ideas:

Learning Area	Resources Required
Personal, social and emotional development	E.g., role play toys
Communication, language and literacy	E.g., flash cards, literacy tapes and work books
Mathematical development	E.g., shapes and colours templates and logic blocks
Knowledge and understanding of the world	E.g., camera, science kits and/or basic model kits and posters
Physical development	E.g., different types of balls, bats and music tapes for dance
Creative development	E.g., paints, drawing materials and coloured paper

Of course the greatest resource that is there for you and your child is the resources of the world. To develop a concern for the planet and the universe is very important, for it will be one of the biggest issues that the next generation (and present) have to address. So before we look at the natural resources, let's identify why the earth has to be studied, and how we might understand the earth's harmony and therefore our own.

Your child's study of the environment must be based on the fact that the earth has a natural harmony, that natural systems are interconnected. So you should introduce them with issues such as:

- Global warming - Global warming is creating disasters in the world. The effect of this means that heat is trapped in the air and causes extreme weather conditions.
- Deforestation - The continued cutting down of forests is changing the temperature of the earth.
- Food Shortages - 40% of the world's agricultural soils have now been degraded due to inappropriate agricultural methods.
- Water - 20% of the world's population do not have access to clean drinking water.
- Hunger - 840 million people in the world are malnourished.
- Exploitation of Natural Resources - Exploitation of water supplies has now resulted in devastating food shortages for many communities.

The concern for the environment should be developed in the home. You should consider recycling your 'waste', and using only environmentally friendly products, and your child should be taught about local animal habitats. Do some research and investigate the natural cycles that impact on your life. On walks ask your child where they think the moon goes during the day, or where the birds go in winter, or how many planets there are in the solar system. For all children, especially young children you can make up funny little stories giving human personalities to the animal characters. The power of the story must be used to teach.

The art of story telling must be married to the world of science. In Euzan Palcy's film *Rue Cases Negres* (1984), an old man by the name of Medouza, tries to teach a young boy life skills. He does this by giving him Crick Crack riddles to work out. The child is excited and entertained. To excite and entertain your child, using the story, all you have to do is simply follow these stages:
1) Work out your plot/story line (keep it simple!)
2) Give the animals or stars etc a name and character type, e.g., the Moon might be called the *Goddess of the Night.*
3) Use the natural habitat that your child can relate to in order to work out the setting. Also, try and get them to imagine other habitats.
4) Realism - use the realism that your child is familiar with which will be that from his/her story books that tend to be magical, and perhaps try and use other cultural realisms, e.g., Anancy stories, folklore, cultural songs/music.
5) Listen to talking books, and collect music that creates a good ambience for story-telling.

In your storytelling you should use mime, music, song, puppets, mimicry etc. Many people don't realise that they have great storytelling traditions in their family and extended family. Think of the uncle or aunt, at a family gathering, or one of your grandparent stories. If you have the opportunity observe them, and then practice yourself by simply reading stories to your child and then ad lib. So many great children's writers started by writing stories for their children. There may be a great children's book in you but the only way to find out is to start writing. Do it!

Remember, practice this great art form and unlock one of your hidden talents.

Learning Through Play

Children learn through play and this approach is much in vogue but this play has to be thought out and researched. Building blocks, art work materials, water play, table toys and books all stimulate learning but this approach must be handled carefully with the parent-teacher aware of aims and objectives, whilst not interfering too much in the child's play.

Play can be seen as the child experimenting. This play-experimenting can take many forms. The child can play as part of a group, or quietly sitting by themselves. In all cases they are engaging with their environment and using their senses (smell, taste, touch, hearing and sight).

As a parent-teacher you will need to get a good balance between planned play activities and unplanned play activities. Their play might be make-believe, involve imaginary characters, real objects, boisterous, obscure, but you should try and simply observe, taking down relevant and discrete notes to later devise other play activities. This will also be useful in formulating your child's learning style which we will look at later.

Your child's play area should be safe, colourful, and well resourced. Have resources for a multi-sensory experience and a place of discovery. For the latter to happen you will have to make discrete changes to the play area, by bringing in resources that the child can engage with using touch, listening, movement etc.

What is the National Curriculum

It's important that the parent knows the curriculum that governs the structure of their child's education. The National Curriculum was introduced in 1988. The curriculum has three core subjects which are compulsory for schools to teach. These subjects are: English, mathematics and science. The curriculum is divided into four key stages: key stage 1, key stage 2, key stage 3 and key stage 4.

Assessment

The National Curriculum tests and exams are called Standard Attainment Targets and help to monitor pupil progress and overall school performance.

Key Stage	Age	Subjects	Test/Exam	Grading
1	7			Eight levels
2	11	English, maths and Science	Standard Attainment Targets (SATs)	That show
3	14	English, Maths and Science, History, Geography, a Modern Language, Design and Technology, Art, Music and PE		Standard and exceptional performance
4	16	(As above)	GCSE	A - G grades, A being the highest

The National Literacy Strategy

Literacy concerns the skills needed in reading, writing speaking and listening. The National Literacy & Numeracy Strategy sets out teaching objectives for Reception to Year 6 to enable students to become fully literate and numerate. Information and Computer Technology (ICT), Black history, and financial literacy must now be considered to be a basic skill and/or a core subject in the curriculum, so you should get your child linked up to an educational website to undertake courses in e-learning.

Below is a summary of the range of work your child should cover in each year.

Reception Year - Literacy (Pre-school)

Fiction and poetry: a variety of traditional, nursery and modern rhymes, poetry and stories with easily recognisable structures and patterned language.
Non-Fiction: simple non-fiction tests, including recounts.

Reception Year - Numeracy (Pre-school)

Say and use number names; count up to 10; recognise numerals to 10; use language to express more, less, greater etc; find one number more or less from 1 - 10; use language to describe shape, size and solid shapes; use language to describe position; mathematical ideas and methods to solve practical problems.

Year 1 - Literacy (Kindergarten)

Fiction and poetry: stories with familiar settings; stories and rhymes.
Non-fiction: signs, labels, captions, lists, instructions.

Year 1 - Numeracy (Kindergarten)

Count 20 objects; count on and back in ones and tens; read, write and order numbers to 20; use vocabulary of comparing and ordering; understand addition, subtraction (take away); know pairs of numbers to 10; use strategies to solve problems involving addition, subtraction, halving & doubling; compare lengths, masses, capacity and mass; describe 3-D and 2-D shapes.

Year 2 - Literacy (Grade 1)

Fiction and poetry: stories, rhymes; fairy tales, stories, poems and plays.
Non-fiction: dictionaries; alphabetically ordered texts and explanantions.

Year 2 - Numeracy (Grade 1)

Count, read, write and order whole numbers to 100; number sequences (know odd and even); know addition and subtraction facts at least to 10; do mental calculations; know how to halve numbers; know 2 & 10 tables; estimate length, mass, capacity using standard units; use a ruler to draw and measure; know 2 & 3D shapes; use mathematical vocabulary to describe position, direction and movement.

Year 3 - Literacy (Grade 2)

Fiction and poetry: Stories, plays, poems and shape poems.
Non-fiction: information texts, dictionaries, letters and encyclopaedias.

Year 3 - Numeracy (Grade 2)

Read, write and order whole numbers to 1000; count back in tens and hundreds; know addition and subtraction facts to 20; know 2 ,5 & 10 x tables; know division is opposite of multiplication; use units of time (second, minute hour day etc); know methods of reasoning; identify right angles; understand lines of symmetry; understand simple lists, tables and graphs.

Year 4 - Literacy (Grade 3)

Fiction and poetry: historical stories, short novels, plays, classic and modern poetry and stories from other cultures.
Non-fiction: reports and newspaper articles, information texts, persuasive writing and debates.

Year 4 - Numeracy (Grade 3)

Use mathematical symbols correctly; round a number to the nearest 100 or 1000; recognise simple fractions, mixed numbers; understand place value; carry out column addition; know 2,3,4,5 & 10 x tables; know division facts from these tables; find remainders after division; know units of length, mass & capacity; classify polygons; use calculations to solve problems.

Year 5 - Literacy (Grade 4)

Fiction and poetry: novels, poems and stories by important children's writers. Myths, legends, narrative poetry and performance poetry.
Non-fiction: news reports; instructional texts (recipes), persuasive writing and dictionaries.

Year 5 - Numeracy (Grade 4)

Multiply or divide any positive interger by up to 10,000 by 10 & 100; order numbers; use decimals; round numbers to 2 decimal places; relate fractions to division and decimals; perform column addition and subtraction (less than 10,000); know multiplication facts up to 10x10; perform multiplication and division; perform long multiplication; understand area measure; understand properties of rectangles; use addition, multiplication, division and subtraction to solve problems.

Year 6 - Literacy (Grade 5)

Fiction and poetry: classic fiction, poetry, drama and Shakespeare; longer novels from different genres (mystery, sci-fi etc); a range of poetic forms; comparison of work by different children's authors.
Non-fiction: autobiography, letters, journalistic writing, formal writing, dictionaries.

Year 6 - Numeracy (Grade 5)

Know about decimals; know about fractions; know about percentages; solve problems using ratio and proportion; carry out column addition and subtraction; perform multiplication; know tables up to 10x10; calculate perimeter; know about coordinates; use operations to solve problems; know about tables, graphs and charts.

Remember, that whilst the National Curriculum offers structured guidelines to follow, the parent-teacher needs to create their own cultural curriculum that might incorporate:
• History
• Religion
• Language

- Literature
- Art
- Science

The purpose of this is to create a curriculum that will give your child respect for their culture, raise their self-esteem and put their education in a real context, that is, to reinforce to them that the purpose of their education is to help build a decent society and express their culture in so doing.

The National Curriculum (in England) or the dominant curriculum of your child's school has meant that publishing houses, wanting greater profits, are producing more and more standardised teaching materials, which serve to test, select, diagnose, assess and grade the student. In some ways this is changing the role of the teacher to more of an educational manager, whereby they simply deliver these teaching materials which are so prescriptive that they determine the delivery, performance criteria, response, outcomes etc, but above all they emphasise student individualism. How the child functions in a group is celebrated less and less in education. Some would say that the teacher has now been deskilled, whilst others might argue that they have simply been reskilled. These dominant curricular which are supported by the big publishing houses focus on testing student's individual competencies in specific skills as opposed to the teaching and testing of human group qualities like sharing, caring and counselling.

The dominant curricular enables local and national governments to set standards/rules that produce students with desired technological and administrative knowledge needed for a modern economy, where teaching materials and knowledge are all packaged like fast food. The learning experience becomes predictable and not centred round the child's talent. However, the parent teacher is uniquely placed to provide an alternative curriculum alongside the curriculum of the school which differs in form and content to that of the 'dominant' curriculum. This is the curriculum of genuis, a curriculum that teaches the child to be critical, creative and address the real pressing issues of the day like poverty, underdevelopment and illiteracy.

This curriculum must respond to the needs of the community from which the child comes from and the community where the school is located. The work achieved by the child on this curriculum should be accredited by the school. This acknowledgement and accreditation by the school of this work should be part of the schools democracy, and indeed the local community's democracy. This genius curriculum has to respond to issues within the community regarding their everyday experience such as marriage, family, diet and economics. With such a community inspired curriculum, there is investment, which is repaid by the student in their eventual support and concern for the local affairs of their community. This is not always the case with the national curricular.

The Teaching Strategy

As a parent-teacher you have to have a range of teaching strategies at your disposal which you can use to teach your child. Below is a list of teaching strategies (Minton 1997).

The teaching strategies range from those which have limited child control to those which have a great deal of child control.

Less Student Control

- Demonstration
- Discussion - structured
- Discussion - unstructured
- Practical

Shared control between Parent-Teacher and child

- Simulation and games
- Role-play
- Resourced-based learning
- Films/TV programmes
- Visits

More Child/Student Control

Distance learning/Flexistudy
Discovery projects/research
Real-life experience

I have found role-play to be a great learning tool as it taps into the creativity of the child. All you have to do is devise a scenario, provide a few props and give some clear aims of the role-play. What you are doing is allowing the child to use visualisation and bring in elements of their 'child's' world. Sometimes toys can take away the creativity of a child, and this is why they'll play with the box that the toy came in as this allows their imagination to have a role in creating something.

The Timetable

You should encourage your child to undertake at least half an hour of formal study in the morning and forty-five minutes in the evening, Monday to Friday. Weekends might see more creative learning focusing on the cultural curriculum.

Each lesson should start with a recap of the previous lesson. Ensure your child looks over the last piece of work they completed.

The Timetable

Days	Mon	Tues	Wed	Thurs	Fri	Sat	Sun
Morning	30min Maths	30mins English	30mins Science	30mins Maths	30mins English		30mins Culture
Evening	30mins Maths	30mins English	30mins Science	30mins Maths	30mins English	Activity /visit	Activity /visit

If your child is going to sit an exam then you will have to devise a revision timetable similar to the one above. Whatever timetable you use set it to suit your schedule. Build in surprises and rewards to the timetable, always remembering that *routine* is the key to a stable home learning environment.

The Lesson Plan

One of the most basic tools when it comes to teaching your child is the lesson plan. The lesson plan outlines the aims of the lesson, the structure, the resources needed, time taken to complete the lesson and the desired outcomes. You should get into the habit of keeping your lesson plans, reviewing and revising them and evaluating them. Below is a model lesson plan that you might wish to use. However, whilst lesson plans are necessary, do not make them restrict you. Great lessons allow for improvisation. The art of teaching is to look for the spark of interest that will allow you access to the child's mind and creativity. The timetable and lesson plan will give you a basic structure but it is the unpredictability that will engage your child. Some parents might not feel able to complete a formal lesson plan, in which case they can use this model to make a simple one that shows topic, time, main aim and resources. I have provided a model which might look technical but you should simplify it, if necessary, so that you have a lesson plan you are comfortable with.

Many years ago when I was an undergraduate I attended a African-Caribbean writers workshop at London University, given by the Jamaican poet John Figeroa. To my surprise, when I walked into the classroom, I saw a man with a long white beard and hair, dancing to calypso music, and half shouting at all of us to, 'dance man, dance!'. It was such a sight. Also in the room were streams of African cloth, all with different colourful designs. At the time I couldn't see the connection, other than to give us a sense of Africa and the Caribbean, but it was enjoyable nonetheless. He had a rich Jamaican accent, striking appearance, and his sleeves were rolled up, thus giving me the impression that the work of the writer was that of a craftsman/woman; something that I would never forget. As a teacher he gave a performance. Later, he explained to me and the other students that he wanted us to get a sense of texture and rhythm in the language of the writers we were to study. His workshops were exciting, stimulating and an adventure. He made learning fun. The greatest learning in a human's life takes place between 0-7 years. It is here that we have great determination, a positive attitude, observation and often observe without discrimination. So make your teaching an adventure for your child. Make it a performance, make it a journey and make it an act of liberation.

Ebony's Example of a Lesson Plan

Lesson Plan for Pre-School (3 - 4)
Term 1   Duration: 50 minutes   Lessons 1 & 2
Aims:
1. To be able to follow the dots to make simple letters and words
2. To have satisfactory hand control in writing simple letters
3. To be able to write and recognise the letters of their name

Topic	Tutor Activity	Child Activity	Outcome(s)
Dot to dot (10 mins)	Show child correct pencil grip. Demonstrate how to go over the dots.	Child draws over dot to dot patterns.	To improve hand eye co-ordination.
Child's name (5 mins)	Tutor writes child's name. Each letter to be spoken aloud as it is written.	Child to say each letter of his/her name.	To become familiar with the letters of his/her name.
Alphabet (10 mins)	Introduce letters of the alphabet using Ebony materials.	Child to repeat the letters read out to them. Draws over the letters with their fingers.	To become familiar with the alphabet. Learn left to right sequence.
Counting Skills (10 mins)	Introduce numbers 1-10. Discover numbers in the child's world, eg the child's DOB, door number etc	Child repeats the numbers. Draws over the numbers with their fingers	To become familiar with numbers 1-10.
Reading (10 mins)	Read a few pages of the black empowerment book. Ask child questions about pictures.	Listens to story. Talks about the picture	Develop language, reading and listening skills.

Homework (Mark previous weeks homework if applicable)	Set and explain homework, plus demonstration.	Look and listen.	To complete homework on sounds and number skills
Review	Check child's understanding with demonstration and questions.	Responds to tutor prompts.	To assess child's attainment.

It might well be impractical for the parent-teacher to devise such lesson plans in the hectic life of the home, but the above lesson plan will act as a guide and model. You can improvise and have a simple bullet point lesson plan that reminds you what areas you want covered and what means of assessment you will use etc.

A Poetical Gift to You from the Tree

The Learning Tree

Pendulum of my people, I swang;
Anchored by the plunge of ancient roots;
Until my peace saw their Gods.

Soon books imprisoned my ignorance;
Foreign clergy stained my papyrus;
I, dumb to this knowledge of hate.

Illiterate I, crawled amongst blind alphabet:
Feeding on poverty and unknown words:
Yes me, the abandoned sinned fruit.

First I stoned the flight of Greek legends;
Chiselled broken history from bare stone;
Made art though I was ignorant of art.

Did they know the taste of yams and plantain?
Had they suckled the knowledge of the bush?
Learnt from angels, elves, and fertility dolls.

Now, I sit amongst magic moon-petals;
Under my peoples' tree, contemplating martyrdom;
Before my Diaspora's court.

Waiting for Nature's muse;
And the fruits of our need;
Waiting for the divine season of our Learning Tree.

Stage 1- Educational Resources: your child's curriculum, health and learning

Key words: resourcefulness, health and vitality

Aims:
- To introduce parents to the needs of their child's brain.
- To give opportunities to the parent-teacher to explore movement and learning.
- To encourage the parent-teacher to reflect on their child's diet.
- To make the parent-teacher aware that their health and their child's health is the foundation for their child's learning.
- To introduce parents to different approaches to research

African Proverb

If you can't hold children in your arms, please hold them in your heart
Ethiopia

In this section we will look carefully at the resources that you will need to function successfully as a parent-teacher, and when we say resources we don't simply mean materials but we also have to include the health of the parent-teacher. There will also be a look at the study space, and the general learning environment to see what you can do to make this space as conducive to learning.

Over the years, every time I have gone in to a school and looked into primary school classrooms I am always amazed at how cluttered and untidy the classrooms are. This isn't the teacher's fault, for it is common practice to have a wide variety of resources crammed into every corner of the classroom. Often, but quite unwittingly perhaps, they create a space where children can escape the teacher's attention and/or be easily distracted.

So let us look at the education resources needed to unlock your child's genius.

Educational Management in the Home: Investigation and Strategy

Educational Management in the Home
The Home as Study Centre - The Study Space
Do you have a quiet space where your child studies regularly? Yes / No
Is the space well ventilated?
Do you have positive statements (affirmations) displayed in this study space? Yes / No
Is this space culturally rich? That is, does it have displays or artworks that give positive representation of your cultural group and that of others?

My action points:
1.
2.
3.

Ebony's suggestion: It is important that this study space is quiet, tidy and well resourced. You should have a filing system and the child should know the rules regarding tidying up. The television must not be allowed to disturb the child working. Preferably the television should be turned off whilst the child is working.

Educational Resources in the Home
1. Do have a book and video library in your home which your child uses for educational purposes?
2. Do you have a music library/collection in your home which your child uses for educational purposes?
3. Do you have a computer in your home which your child uses for educational purposes?

My action points:
1.
2.
3.

Ebony's suggestion:
Use the internet to access important educational websites that focus on educational information and advice, educational resources and educational opportunities.

The Television

Do you monitor what your child watches on television? Yes / No
Do you plan what your child watches in advance? Yes / No
Do you buy educational videos for your child to watch?

Action points:
1.
2.
3.

Ebony's suggestion:
Encourage your child to watch the science and nature programmes on television. Respond to these programmes by bringing something that reflects the natural world into the home.

The Story

Do you read stories to your child?
Do you buy story books or audio books for your child?

My action points:
1.
2.
3.

Ebony's suggestion:
The story is a powerful tool which can give your child the love of learning and introduce them to experiences they would otherwise not have. Introduce them to a range of reading material. If they are at present a poor reader then get them books that they can easily manage to boost their confidence. Try to read to your child each night, and hear them read everyday for about 15 minutes.

Education and Culture

Do you take your child to see a major cultural event like a play, exhibition or festival at least once per term? Yes / No
Have you encouraged your child's school to undertake a cultural event project? Yes / No
Do you celebrate any cultural events in the home like International Women's Week, Black History Month etc? Yes / No

My action points:
1.
2.
3.

Ebony's suggestion:
The home is one of the few opportunities that you have to give positive representation of multicultural society, history and the black experience. Take your child to major cultural events but jointly engage in some research before the event if necessary.

Your Child's School

Do you attend parents' evening each term/year? Yes/No
What strategy have you devised for improving your child's educational experience?

My action points:
1.
2.
3.

Ebony's suggestion:
Unfortunately many children have a negative or limiting experience in school. Whether this is the case or not, identify your child's individual educational plan; strategies for improving their self esteem and take advantage of any extra curricular activities.

Home Environment

Is the home quiet and relaxed? Yes / No

The 'yes' answers will indicate that you have addressed this area to some extent, and the 'no' answers will indicate that you need to focus on this particular area.

About eight years ago, one languid Spring day, a mother came to me to ask for advice on how best she could help her child who was underachieving. She was a determined, attractive woman but slightly hurried in her appearance, which also gave away the fact that she was a successful businesswoman. She explained the problems she was having with the boy, which included stubborness, truancy and a disinterest in his schooling. She spoke with a determined Jamaican accent, revealing that she was a self-made businesswoman who was worn down by the dual projects of trying to run a successful business and bring up a boy, who was on the brink of being a teenager. She invited me to her home which I visited her one evening. Her house was large, and plush, from where she also ran her business. It was there that I met her son. I was immediately struck by his sleepy eyes, sluggish gait and sensed that he needed attention. We talked about his education for a while, whilst he walked in and out of the room, wary of me and becoming increasingly uneasy. Some time afterwards she showed me around the large house. Eventually, we came to his bedroom and there on the floor were several large crates of fizzy drinks. He had a television, computer games, the latest furniture and clothes. His room was full of resources but the wrong kind. She had simply pampered him to quell his outbursts.
Straight away I could see what was causing his sleepy eyes. A few minutes later we went back downstairs to the lounge, where I fed back to her what educational services I could offer, ideas and strategies that she could use in the home and in particular measures she should consider in addressing his obvious dietary needs. She was surprisingly naïve about his diet but nonetheless, very receptive to the ideas I presented her with regarding her child attending one of our education

projects and seeing a nutritionist. I got to know the boy quite well after a few months and began to see why his mother was having difficulties dealing with his behavioural problems. He was at the pre-adolescent stage where he was beginning to challenge her authority, the school authority and enter this adolescent world without a father figure. His mother, like so many other mothers who come to our projects and who are themselves often from female one parent households, always request that their child be put in a class with a male teacher. This request also comes from our female teachers who note that the boys are better behaved when there is a male teacher teaching them. Research also shows that boys who have a strong father figure in their lives are less likely to be involved in crime. The point I make here is that this mother in addressing his pre-adolescence behaviour, simply tried to pamper him but what he needed in addition to a diet regime was guidance on his growing masculinity. The mother, unintentionally, was sedating his burgeoning masculinity with drinks and expensive toys and games. A male role model was needed. This role might be met by uncles, close male friends and supported by boy-to-men life skills programmes.

Do You Have the Health to Be a Parent-Teacher?

This education programme demands that the parent-teacher optimises their health. The foundation to any health regime is to undertake a detoxification course. I encourage the parent-teacher to seek a recommended programme but for now, here is a basic detox plan.

What is detoxification?

Detoxification is the elimination of potentially harmful chemicals (toxins) from the body. You are constantly in contact with toxins everyday such as pollutants, pesticides, household chemicals, toxic metals (lead and mercury) and food additives etc. Luckily your body is designed to cope with the demands of detoxing through the kidneys, liver, gut, skin and lungs. However, the detoxification process demands that the body has enough nutrients to carry out this process. The liver in particular has to work hard to detoxify the body.

How Does the Toxic State Occur?

Food residue and mucous form in the colon and small intestines. Much of the fecal waste can't be eliminated by normal bowel movement. If the fecal stays in the body you will suffer from autointoxication.

Useful information for your detox plan

1) Detox your home with space clearing; i.e., a general spring clean whilst throwing out old clothes and things that you have stored but never used. You might wish to burn frankincence, say prayers, bless your home etc.

2) Identify potential toxins in your diet and environment, e.g. coffee, fried food, alcohol, smoking etc.
3) Identify possible symptoms of toxicity (flatulence, bloating, depressions, haemorrhoids, skin disorders etc).
4) Drink water (6-8 glasses) and herbal teas each day. The last day of your detox should be water only.
5) Eat raw organic food only.
6) Take detox supplements and food like milk thistle, garlic, broccoli, vitamin C, methionine, dandelion root, echinacea.
7) Introduce foods that detox your system as part of your normal diet. You may also wish to invest in a detox recipe book.

What Are the Benefits of a Detox Plan?

1) Greater clarity of mind.
2) More energy.
3) Possible relief from symptoms like flatulence, bloating, depression, irritability etc.
4) The maintenance of overall good health.
5) Improved sleep quality.

Summary outline of foods that assist in the detoxification process.

Food/Vitamin	Detoxification Effect
Artichokes	Helps the flow of bile
Raw beetroots	Helps the regeneration of the liver
Raw broccoli, brussel sprouts and cabbage	Supports the liver detoxification process
Dandelion root	Increases the flow of bile
Echinacea and Sarspirilla	Supports the lymphatic circulation which acts like a drainage system
Epsom bath salts (in the bath)	Supports lymphatic circulation
Garlic and onion	Helps in the elimination of harmful heavy metals from the body
Methionine	Helps to regulate fat metabolism and increase the flow of bile
Milk Thistle	Assists in liver cell regeneration
Vitamin C	An antioxidant which fights against free radicals

Stress Management of the Parent-Teacher

In order to support your child's education you have to make sure that your lifestyle is stress free. What is stress? Stress is a lifestyle where there is worry, tension and continued reaction to situations. Here the nervous system is sending blood to the muscles to ensure peak physical performance, but the vital organs (kidneys, liver etc) and brain, are denied this blood and therefore under-perform. Stress management for the parent-teacher requires a lifestyle change. You can help yourself to cope with stress by taking the following:

a)   Learn a breathing exercise, e.g., pranayama yoga breathing
b)   Drink 6 to 8 glasses of bottled water per day
c)   Do a simple aerobic exercise every morning
d)   Vitamin C (500 /day)
e)   B Complex
f)   Eat raw food (at least 50-70% of your food should be raw organic)
g)   Avoid taking sugar and salt in large quantities
h)   L-glutamine and L-tyrosine
i)   A good multi vitamin and mineral supplement

Your Child's Brain

The brain weighs about three pounds, has two hemispheres, uses up a tremendous amount of oxygen and has one trillion neurons (brain cells). The job of the neuron is to send, store and receive information. You can stimulate the brain through movement, play, music etc which creates chemical messengers called neurotransmitters.

The brain needs nutrients. Give your child and yourself nutritious food. This ensures that your brain has the correct brain chemistry. Make sure your child exercises daily and does some form of active sport or aerobic exercise.

Vital to the health and performance of your child's brain are long chain fatty acids which is found in breast milk and oily fish. These particular fatty acids belong to the omega-3 family. Omega-3 and Omega-6 foods should be consumed in balance. These fatty acids are known as arachiodonic acid (AA) and docosahexaenoic acid (DHA) which play an important role in the structure of the brain tissue. AA and DHA are particularly important in infancy for the nervous system, vision and cognition. DHA helps keep the nerve cells in good physical condition. Two other acids which are important to the brain's functions are eicosapentaenoic (EPA) and dihomogamma-linolenic (DGLA). These longchained polyunsaturated (LCPs) acids enable the brain to send messages and store information. LCPs can be made in the body from essential fatty acids from alpha linoleic acid (ALA) which is found in flaxseeds and walnuts. The above information is also good guidance for the parent-teacher in terms of the their own necessary brain food.

Movement and Learning

Make sure your child does physical activities that involve spinning, jumping, running, fun, balancing and physical activities as these all stimulate the brain and inner ear motion, developing neural pathways that make for an efficient brain that can readily learn. Such physical activities will improve your child's spatial perception, language skills, emotional stability and memory.

The main aim of movement and learning programmes like *Brain Gym* are to stimulate the frontal lobes where higher order thinking takes place. Body movement stimulates the core muscles, which stimulates the vestibular system (inner ear and balance system), which then stimulates other parts of the brain (cerebellum and amygdala) which connect to the frontal lobes. The parent-teacher should therefore stop their child from leading a sedentary lifestyle where the child simply sits and watches television, or plays computer games and gets driven everywhere.

Lunch Box or Lunch Bomb?

During the last 17 years since I've been running educational projects, I've seen hundreds of children walk in with lunch boxes that should really be called lunch bombs, for they contained bars of chocolate, packets of crisps full of salt and various brightly coloured fizzy drinks. Despite providing literature from established authorities highlighting the dangers of these diets, some parents still give their children this type of food, ignorant of how poor diet can not only undermine their child's educational performance, but also ignorant of the serious illnesses that will lie in wait for their child if they continue to feed them this diet.

A recent study (Jeffery, 2004) shows that 33% of mothers and 57% of fathers describe their obese children as normal. This study shows that many parents simply do not recognise abnormal weight gain in their own children. Also worrying is that obesity can lead to type 2 diabetes and other health issues. So we can see the importance of the parent-teacher tackling the diet of the child and home.

A Brief Health Plan for Your Child Might Contain the Following:

➢ Make sure they drink several glasses (5-6) of water each day. Water helps in the absorption of oxygen, improves cell activity, thereby assisting learning.
➢ Make sure they do activities that involves aerobics. Aerobic activity again increases oxygen to the brain.
➢ Movement and exercise. Movement stimulates the neural network in your child and exercise strengthens the muscular system, immune system and the lungs.

Useful Information for Your Child's Nutritional Plan

A healthy diet for your child consists of water, carbohydrate, protein, fats, vitamins, minerals and fibre. Your child's nutritional plan should be based around three nutritional meals a day and perhaps two healthy snacks. It is also recommended that children eat five portions of fruit and vegetables each day. A balanced diet should provide your child with the following:

Carbohydrates

Carbohydrates (starches and sugars) provide the body with energy and warmth. Carbohydrate foods include rice, cereals, pasta and breads.

Protein

Protein (composed of amino acids) is vital for the body to repair, build and maintain its tissues and cells. It is extremely important for the growth of children. Protein foods include meat, fish, pulses, soya, nuts and seeds. Protein is also vital during periods of growth in infancy and adolescence, or in times of illness and infection. For children on vegetarian and vegan diets a wide variety of protein foods is important to ensure they receive all the necessary amino acids for growth.

Fats

Fats are either saturated or polyunsaturated. Saturated fat, is high in cholesterol and can cause health problems. Polyunsaturated fats have low cholesterol, cannot be produced by the body, are important for good health and are found in foods such as seeds, soya, nuts and oily fish. Fats are energy foods and are important for children.

Vitamins

Vitamins are essential for good health and are found in plants and animals. Most vitamins, (except for vitamin D and K) have to be taken through food. Their main purpose is to support enzyme activity and when absent from the diet can lead to health disorders.

Minerals

Minerals are taken into the body when we eat cereals, plants, fruit, vegetables and water. They also assist in enzyme activity and are important in strengthening bones and teeth, and in the regulation of body fluids and enzyme activity.

Dietary Fibre

Dietary fibre is made up of the fibrous structure of vegetables, cereals and fruit. Dietary fibre is not digested but is important in aiding digestion and absorption of food. It helps bowel health and prevents constipation.

Water

Water makes up 76% of body weight. It is vital in the oxygen uptake of haemo-globin. Water contains the minerals sodium and potassium, which along with the kidneys play an important role in the fluid balance in the body. It is an important part of all body cells and also helps carbon dioxide, glucose and salt in their transportation between body cells and blood vessels.

The National Diet and Nutrition Survey in June 2000 found the following trends in children's diet:

- Children only ate two portions of vegetables and fruit per day.
- Children in low income families were 50% less likely to eat fruit and vegetables.
- The amount of fruit and vegetables children eat has fallen since 1983.
- One in five children do not eat fruit in a single week.
- School children have diets that are dependent on foods containing high levels of sugars, fat and salt.

We can see from the above information that one way to address this situation is for the parent and child to become aware of the benefits of a healthy diet.

Food in the Home

For young children, food in the home can be a way to further developing a range of skills as food brings children together, thereby exercising and developing their skills in co-operation and sharing. Food provides ways to experience other cultures as long as the parent prepares further activities to allow the child opportunities to engage in the culture from where the food/recipe originated from. For the young child, the safe preparation of food will help develop their mathematical skills in weighing, sharing, mixing, measuring and problem solving. Above all, it will develop health awareness in the child.

Allergies

The parent-teacher should also be aware of foods that cause allergies. The seven foods that cause 90% of allergic reactions are:
- Milk
- Wheat
- Peanuts
- Soya
- Tree Nuts
- Fish
- Shellfish

Gluten insensitivity should also be mentioned. Gluten is contained in cereals and can produce bloatedness and diarrhoea. Some years ago we had one of our children exhibiting extreme hyperactivity. We suggested to the parents that they consult a nutritionist who eliminated gluten from the child's diet. The hyperactivity stopped almost immediately. Not all experts agree that hyperactivity is linked to diet but my experience is that this is the case.

The Learning Space and Feng Shui

You will need to create a clean and tidy space where your child can study if you don't have one already. This space must be peaceful and conducive to learning. Feng Shui (pronounced fung shway) has been used since ancient times in China to help create harmonious living spaces. The discipline is a way of life. Feng Shui considers everything in the environment to have energy lines (chi/life force) which flow through the environment. Therefore, arranging all your belongings can bring positive energy (chi) to your surroundings.

Some key points regarding feng shui and education that you should consider are:

- Education Feng Shui is symbolised by the direction north-east (the trigram Ken). You should therefore seek to have your study area in the north-east part of the house, if this is practically possible.
- The element that is used to symbolise north-east (trigram Ken) is earth.
- Items used to symbolise earth are natural crystals.
- The crystal should be placed on the desk.
- Clay and pottery are also earth symbols
- The study table should be placed at the north-east direction of the room.
- The student's back should not face the door.
- Four items which are seen to be very auspicious when they are placed in the study space are: ink, a brush pen, a sheet of good quality paper and an ink slab.

Zen Interior Design

By looking at Zen interior design we can get ideas on how to be minimalist (use as little furnishings as possible) and effectively utilise space in the home in which we want to create a study area.

The two main elements to Zen interiors in terms of style are serenity and simplicity, which is achieved by creating a harmonious environment that in turn creates balance. Zen thought warns against having too much possessions as this will work against the freedom of the spirit. A typical Zen interior, which will greatly enhance the learning space, will have simple walls and floors in white and light colours. So essentially the Zen learning space should consist of:

- Simple walls, floors and objects
- Create harmony and balance with colours, straight line features; discreet use of light and shade, house plants and meditative music to create a relaxing ambience.
- The Zen space allows for a multi-sensory experience, so the discreet use of glass, stone, pottery and bamboo can add to the healing affect of the space.
- Use mirrors to reflect light, use colour to create moods.
- Use light to keep the learning space well lit and well ventilated, and to counter the effects of computers and their electric field.

Creating the Allergy Free Learning Space

With so many children having different forms of allergies we should consider taking precautions in creating an allergy free learning space so that it does not interfere with your child's learning.

An allergy is a condition which is induced by allergens affecting the immune response of the body. The most common conditions are:
- Hay fever
- Asthma
- Rhinitis
- Eczema
- Urticaria

The most widespread allergens in the home are associated with:
- House dust mites
- Pets
- Cockroaches
- Mould allergens
- Dampness in the home

You should therefore take precautionary measures and seek expert advice if you feel that your child has an allergy.

The ideal study space for your child should consist of:
- Minimal furniture
- Hard-surface flooring (wood or vinyl floors etc) to prevent moulds
- Walls should be kept plain and simple
- Windows should have roller blinds, or vertical blinds to prevent dust collecting
- The computer should be turned off when not in use

The above measures will help to stop your child from aggravating any allergies they might have but further measures to your child's bedding might be necessary such as:
- Don't use padded headboards
- A raised bed is preferable as this helps with effective cleaning under the bed
- The mattress should be covered with dust proof covering
- Use anti-mite barrier covers on all bedding
- Vacuum your child's room regularly

Research for the Parent Teacher

Throughout this book the parent teacher will be asked to conduct research so that they become better informed about their child's education.

Types of research

Psychologists use both formal (experiments and case studies) and informal re search methods. Throughout this book I will be encouraging you, the parent-teacher, to undertake informal research regarding your child. Informal research consists of observing your child, listening to their conversations, noting their interest and watching their general behaviour.

However, the parent-teacher should engage in as much research as possible. If you do so you will come across three types of research study:

1. Cross-sectional studies - research that attempts to find evidence from a representative sample of children that something is true for all members of a specific group. E.g., when looking at children's attitudes to aggression or the opposite sex.
2. Longitudinal studies - research conducted over a long period of time to note changes say in behaviour or ideas and attitudes. E.g. when looking at children who have spent all of their lives in an orphanage. They might be studied when they are 7, 14 and 21 years of age.
3. Cross-cultural studies - research conducted on different cultural groups on some aspect of child development. E.g. research on different child-rearing styles and how children develop in different parts of the world.

Further Research for the Parent-Teacher

Research into:
- Theories into child development
- The national curriculum or the dominant curriculum which governs your child's education.

A Poetical Gift from the Tree to You.

People of the Tree

They came to the beyond of our garden
These mythical workers of the world.

Hugs for trees and little animals
As they breathed their celestial air.

Placards grew there too,
Bright blossomed slogans for all to share.

So I wandered into the garden
To play with nature bare.

Workers of the earth unite!
And all about me was their stare.

Braided mermaid's recycled legends

Angels and leprechauns entered in pairs .

And this labour of beings transfixed my soul:
For a Tree was born in my garden there.

Stage 2- Educational Management in the Home: parental skills and learning styles

Key words/themes: memory techniques, nurturing and learning

Aims:
- To make the parent-teacher aware of the need to nurture a positive learning environment.
- To encourage the parent-teacher to reflect on their relationship with their child.
- To encourage the parent-teacher to develop an even greater sensitivity towards their child by exploring their own childhood.
- To introduce the parent-teacher to learning styles and spelling strategies.

African Proverb
Knowledge is like a garden:
if it is not cultivated,
it cannot be harvested
Guinea

Remember your own childhood; the smells, the images surrounding the magic of play. Remember uncles and aunts and relatives, of food; the laughter, the quiet and the mystery. Remember these things, and the innocence of being a child, and with these memories look upon your child. Once you've done this look at your child with no memory or anticipation but simply look at them as if observing them for the first time. Now write down what you see.

Knowing Your Child

Child's Name:
Age:

Likes and Dislikes

- I know exactly what my child likes and dislikes. Yes / No
- I'm unsure what my child likes and dislikes. Yes / No

- **My action points:**
-
-

Suggestion: sit down with your child and talk to them about what they like doing and don't like doing. Put time aside to do (as a family) what they like doing.

Discipline

- When disciplining my child I always make sure that they know I disliked their behaviour but not them. Yes / No
- I have set clear boundaries that my child knows must not be broken.

- **My action points:**

Suggestion: reward good behaviour, achievements and effort with a treat and penalise bad behaviour (without getting angry) for a limited period.

Friends

- I'm quite happy with his/her friends. Yes/No
- I'm not quite happy about his friends. Yes/No

- **My action points:**
-
-

Suggestion: make sure you don't try and pressurise your child into being friends with particular children based on a prejudice. Encourage your child to have a wide range of children as friends.

School

My child is happy in school. Yes No
They have lots of friends. Yes No

My child has a good relationship with his/her teacher. Yes / No
My child hasn't any problems in school like bullying etc. Yes / No
My child is making good progress in school. Yes / No

- **My action points:**
-
-

Suggestion: Make sure that you have an educational action plan for your child.

Outside School Activities

My child has many outside school activities. Yes / No
My child watches more than four hours of TV each day. Yes / No

My child engages in very little creative play. Yes / No

- My action points:
-
-

Suggestion: research into out-of-school activities in the library, on the internet and local leisure centres. Bring creative stimuli into the home, like the Genius Programme and take an interest in the new activity.

Assessing School

Is school a place where all children learn, or where some children learn and some don't? Is it a place where children are assessed, tested, selected and categorised for academic achievement? A place where some children are prepared for skilled work and others prepared for unskilled work based on class and race? Is it a place where children are grouped by age, then ability, and where the main focus of pressurised teachers is on test results which is supposed to indicate school performance? Is your child's school a place where there is strong leadership from the Headteacher or Principal, a place where teachers are involved in decision-making, a place where there are clear goals, innovative teaching and learning; the sincere valuing of pupils cultures and good teacher pupil ratio and relationship? These are just some points that you need to consider in assessing your child's school.

A school is a unique place because you get an number of communities coming 'together' to get what's best for *their* child, or what the parent thinks, and has been told, is best for their child. There is a constant power struggle going on amongst the teachers, governors, education authorities and parents. The parents whose children will lose out the most are those who do not understand the power relations operating in their children's school and in the education system as a whole.

My work as an independent educationalist has meant me addressing the needs of children who are underachieving, and who have had various labels put on them. No single test can assess the ability of the child and testing has been found to be culturally and class biased. It was partly my horrendous school experience that led me to be a teacher and writer. Here is a story about a group of black and ethnic minority boys who were almost destroyed by the education system but managed through their own ingenuity to still keep their dreams of achievement alive.

The Ritual of '74

It wasn't about scoring a goal, or winning a match, or youth football league; no, it was about survival, celebration, identity and defiance. This was our ritual against those who attempted to make us educationally sub-normal. The year was 1974, and we were known as the G boys, for most of us were in the Class 11 G, which meant we were in the bottom class, where all the PE teachers would come unprepared and just make us copy out some meaningless passage from a book they barely knew themselves. It was a hot summer. The summer when we would leave and go out into the world, aspiring to be men. It was June; exams meant little to most of us, for the school had long since given up on us, but we stayed and took the CSE exams partly for our parents who didn't quite understand how their children could have failed so badly. But each lunch-time when we couldn't be bothered to walk through the back streets of Catford to the local girls school, we'd stay in the playground where a fascinating game of football would follow. Each of us had a nick-name. These were names that captured some kind of essence that we saw in each other. There was *Lick-Foot Leroy*, who would kick you with absolutely no intention to get the ball, and would sneer when you ended up on the ground clutching your ankle. There was *Chopper Chambers*, a bigger than average boy, who would MC or toast as we called it in those days as he played, bringing a Jamaican commentary to the play; improvising as he went along, using rhythms and beats from the local sound system The Mighty Jah Shaka. And there were others: *Mash-Up Mickey, Bootsy, Sticks-Bwoy, Deadly-Delroy, Eliott Ness, Rasta-Rebell and Tïef-Ball-Tony*. We assumed a new identity because our identity had been damaged by the teachers, many of whom had been in the army and viewed us as colonials who they had to "break". And this breaking was achieved through detentions, constant reprimands, poor reports, exclusions, ridicule, negative comments and worst of all smirks. So we played this game of ritual football. We had fantastic skills. Whoever had the ball simply dribbled in the style befitting their name; celebrating the identity assigned to them by us their peers; a name that gave them a true identity, self-esteem, peer recognition, and an opportunity for cultural expression. And we knew that the teachers were looking on; we knew they couldn't understand our ritual-football, the reasons why we played the way we did, and how we could still have belief in ourselves after all the humiliation. The structure of the ritual/game was in three parts: *the declaration* that we were proud of who we were, which led to dance steps, then exaggerated boasting and finally, physical posturing. We were becoming young men. The school had no rites of passage programme. We had to invent our own. We knew each time we played that there was some kind of *transformation*. Collectively, we were awakening. After the awakening, the game would reach its heightened state; we would become possessed, possessed by genius. The whereabouts of the ball simply directed the spotlight on each player. Finally there would be *revelation*. We would experience a collective wisdom, an insight into our own genius. The teachers hated this game, because there was no cultural reference to their world. Their education system had made us underachieve but it had not defeated our genius.

Tired and exhausted we would head back into the school building, again under the surveillance of the teachers. For five years we had had to endure their tests, exams, assessments; apparatus for them to reaffirm their alleged normalcy and our otherness. These men assessed us constantly. They could not see genius in our ritual-football, they couldn't see creativity or ingenuity. Our cultural knowledge by which we played football was not legitimate knowledge in their eyes. Another lesson for you, as a parent-teacher, is that the child, especially the teenage child, may well hang out with certain friends, develop interests or even join a gang in search for an "education" that has meaning in their world. This is what the boys of '74 did because they found their educational experience alienating and meaningless.

Their assessment of us as pupils was in the context of surveillance, for we were always being watched for fear of this innate wisdom. It was almost as if they knew the power of our collective expression, which we could only evoke on certain occasions. Children like those of '74, still seek their own cultural youth references to give their educational experience meaning. Parent-teachers have to understand that what the school is assessing might well be the child's class, race, community, lifestyle and function. It is for the community to respond to these inaccurate assessments, that deny cultural knowledge. Your child's assessment is simply limited to specific skills. Don't be distraught if your child's assessment is disappointing. Study methods of assessments used in your child's school; look at the criteria and assess the assessment procedure. Also, once you put a programme together for the unlocking of your child's genius in place, you should be continuously assessing your child's genius and if your child is achieving, then you have to ask why they are not achieving in school. You have to start this journey.

Learning Styles

At this stage you have to passionately devote yourself to the great work of unlocking your child's genius. Now that you have started this wonderful education programme you have to live, breathe and eat education. Tell your friends, relatives and work colleagues that you have started the *Unlocking Your Child's Genius programme*. Your starting point at this stage is to revisit your own education. Give yourself a positive affirmation. For example:

With love and devotion I am unlocking my child's genius.

Make sure that you read this to your child and congratulate yourself for you have planted a seed, so let your Tree take root.

Learning Styles

A learning style is the way in which you learn. Using the VAKT (Visual, Auditory, Kinaesthetic and Tactile) model there are 4 learning styles:
a) Visual
b) Auditory
c) Kinaesthetic
d) Tactile

This means that you and your child learn best using a particular learning style e.g. visual methods, through pictures and images; through listening (auditory); through moving around (kinaesthetic) and tactile (touching). By understanding your child's preferred learning style you can best teach your child.

Here is a short but revealing Learning Styles questionnaire to explore your child's learning style preference.

How to score:
➢ Yes = 2,   No = 1,   Sometimes = 0
➢ You can only enter one score per question
➢ When you have put a score for all the questions in each of the four sections compare the totals and the sections with the highest score will indicate what type of learner you child is.

Visual Learner	Yes	No	Sometimes
My child learns best by observing things?			

My child learns best by watching others?			
My child likes books with bright pictures?			
My child likes to draw and/or read?			
My child likes colourful things?			
Total			

Auditory Learner	Yes	No	Sometimes
My child learns best by listening?			
My child likes listening to music?			
My child listens carefully when I speak to him/her?			
My child gets upset when he/she is not listened to?			
My child listens carefully and can recall details?			
Total			

Kinaesthetic	Yes	No	Sometimes
My child fidgets a lot?			
My child likes to rock in their chair a lot?			
My child can't keep still and keeps moving around?			
My child likes to move around when they are learning?			
My child seems to do things better when they are allowed to move around?			
Total			

Tactile	Yes	No	Sometimes
My child is always touching things?			
My child likes to learn in practical settings?			
My child likes making things?			
My child likes exploring things primarily through touch?			
My child likes to play with toys/games that involve hand skills?			
Total			

My child is a (please circle): visual auditory kinaesthetic tactile learner

The parent should not place too much emphasis on learning styles. The key point to remember is that there should be variety in the learning experience. More importantly (which also ensures variety) there should be improvisation to the lesson plan, and there should be the learning performance initiated by both teacher and pupil. Great importance should be placed on placing the learning style within a cultural context, that is, use images, music/sounds, objects etc that have cultural significance to the learner. This cultural context of learning will allow you to open other doors to your child as you introduce cultural artefacts etc from other cultures which further stimulate the child's learning experience.

Now that you have investigated your child's learning style here are some ideas to now help their learning. Knowing your child's learning preference can help in their learning of spellings and help in the delivery of learning material for children that are dyslexic by encouraging their teacher and parent-teacher to vary the teaching materials. That is, a wide variety of materials should be used like coloured paper, audio tapes, computers, tactile materials and discussion.

Visual Strategies for Spelling

- Use mind maps (explained in Stage 4) with spelling patterns and/or spelling sounds
- Use a highligter to highlight words within words
- Write out the word over a period of 5/7 days and look for patterns
- Use pictures or symbols to help break up the syllables
- Make the spelling unusual in some way through exaggeration so that it stands out in their imagination.

Auditory Strategies for Spelling

- Say the word breaking it up into syllables and listen to the sounds
- Make up a rap
- Use a mnemonic device by using each letter to remember the spelling, e.g., because: big elephants can't all use small exits.
- Play music (60 beats per minute) while your child is learning their spelling.

Kinaesthetic Strategies for Spelling

- Allow your child to move as they say/learn the spellings.
- Write the spellings on pieces of card which can be shuffled and/or carried around and learnt.
- Allow your child to write the words in the air and say each letter as it is written.
- When learning spellings, allow your child to take breaks and/or go for a walk.

Memory, Dreams and Learning

To make an improvement in your child's learning, you have to improve your memory, which means you must improve your personal organisation, make changes to your lifestyle and ensure that you engage in relaxation techniques to aid the performance of your memory. In addition to this you should be aware of yours and your child's learning style. If you don't work on your memory and equip yourself with memory aids you will simply forget about the programme. This programme is a foundation for lifelong learning. Once you consistently remember and engage with this learning programme you will become devoted to unlocking not only your child's, and your genius, but other peoples too. So memory is one of the keys.

How to Improve Your Child's Memory

Tony Buzan's memory technique is quite useful; this memory aid is called, SMASHIN SCOPE, which makes memorising something much easier. The letters stand for:

S - Sensuality
Sensualise, if possible, whatever it is to be memorised.
M - Movement
Create movement in imagination to help with memorising.
A - Association
Our brains excel with association, therefore we should associate an experience with a memory.
S - Sexual Interest
By adding a romantic angle to something you want to remember helps memorising.
H - Humour
Add humour to something you want to memorise.
I - Imagination   N - Numbers

Add fantasy or exaggeration to the thing you want to memorise.

SCOPE

S - Signs
A way of writing graphic short hand for ideas that might be long and complicated.
C - Colours
By using colours you can brighten up, expand and contrast what's to be memorised.
O - Order
You can memorise better by numbering things, putting things in alphabetical order or in some other kind of sequence.
P - Positiveness
Make your memories positive so you enjoy their recall.
E - Exaggeration
Something stands out if it is unusually large or peculiar.

Your Child's Review Timetable

Once a learning session has taken place it is important that a system of review is undertaken to ensure that the information or skill learnt is not forgotten. Notes or the actual work undertaken should be reviewed as follows:

- Ten minutes after the learning session.
- One day after the learning session.
- One week after the learning session.
- One month after the learning session.
- Four months after the learning session.
- When necessary

Buzan recommends, *In Make the Most of Your Head,* that five minutes review for a one hour learning session is sufficient. You should use this system of review when working with this book to ensure that the information this book contains is accessed by your long term memory.

Brain Gym

Brain Gym consists of twenty-six exercises and movements developed by Dr. Paul E Dennison to help children learn. These movements and exercises aim to balance and integrate the whole brain. Brain Gym helps children's memory, concentration, reading and organisational skills. These movements and exercises increase the connections between the various parts of the brain and body. Brain Gym works on the idea that learning is not confined to the brain alone but the whole intelligence (neural network) of the body. Brain Gym is now not only popular in schools but corporate training programmes.

The parent-teacher who wishes to find out more about Brain Gym might wish to go on the internet and find out about training courses in Brain Gym.

Below is a brief summary of some of the exercises and movements and the different areas of learning Brain Gym supports.

Exercise/Movement	Area of Learning
Cross Crawl - child moves opposite legs and arms, and touches knee with opposite hand.	Good for thinking; mathematical skills; feeling positive and self awareness.
Belly Breathing - child places hands on belly and blows all the air out in short breaths. Child then takes in more air, arching back slightly and breathes out.	Good for thinking, mathematics and reading.
Cobra - the child lies belly down on the floor, pretending they are a snake; lifts their head but keeps legs and waist on floor.	Good for concentration and self awareness.
Arm Activation - the child places one arm up in the air next to their ear, holding their elbow with the other hand and pushes held arm to the front, back, out and in.	Good for writing skills.
Brain Buttons - the child places one hand over navel and using thumb and index finger on the other hand massages one inch below collarbone.	Good for reading.

Dreams and Learning

Everyone dreams but not everyone remembers their dreams. Dreams are problem solving devices that allow for review, understanding and warning. Sleep is essential for the body to rejuvenate itself, and during this period of sleep the body goes through a number of rapid eye movement states, and non-rapid eye movement states. The rapid eye movement state occurs an hour after you go to sleep and lasts about 90 minutes. If we look at the different brain waves that the brain has we can at least have some idea how we can create the brain-state that is most conducive to learning.

The five types of brainwaves are:

❖ Alpha occurs as the body enters a deep relaxed state.
❖ Beta occurs when there is intense mental concentration and anxiety.
❖ Theta occurs in a creative and inspirational state.
❖ Delta occurs when there is deep sleep and there is an escape from conscious activity.
❖ Gamma. This state is not entirely understood but it is thought to be similar to the delta state.

To ensure good sleep quality don't take stimulants like tea, coffee or alcohol before you go to sleep. Intensive work with the Genius programme may well lead to the parent-teacher experiencing an insightful dream related to the programme. You should keep a dream diary and note down insights gained into the Genius programme. You should also ensure you and your child get good quality sleep by sleeping in a well ventilated room, making sure that the diet has the right nutritional balance and that the child does not watch media which is disturbing in terms of violence and excessive noise.

Further Research for the parent-teacher

Conduct basic research (short summary notes) into the work of:
- Jean Piaget - Swiss educationalist
- Maria Montessouri - Italian founder of the Montessouri method
- Amos Wilson - African-American educationalist

A Poetical Gift to You From the Tree

Mother

She grew pounding yam;
Smelt the early sex of roast corn,
Hemmed the dresses of the world,
That splashed on the dance floor she scrubbed

In the yard of her youth
She danced with cutlass
Fields still full of slave prayers

And she grew to be our mother and icon.
Woman of bush and bark;
Of chant and magic;
Of black night and healing drum:

Whose wisdom adorns my Learning Tree:
So innocent in the disguised morning.

Stage 3- How Your Child Learns: reading, mathematics and dyslexia

Key words: logic, mathematics and positive affirmations

Aims
- To introduce the parent-teacher to the strategies involved in developing mathematical and reading skills.
- To introduce the parent-teacher to strategies dealing with dyslexia and ADHD
- To introduce to the parent-teacher the need for positive thinking.

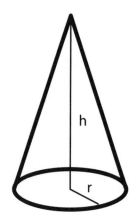
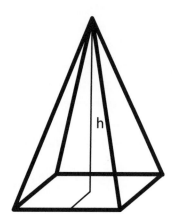

African Proverb

A child who is fearless is going to bring tears to his mother's eyes
Sierra Leone

In order for this programme to be successful you must maintain positive thinking, and to achieve this you must immerse yourself in positive affirmations. Here are some affirmations that you might wish to repeat on a daily basis during this programme:

❖ *I am my child's greatest educator, for I am blessed with great talents.*

❖ *With all my great gifts I am unlocking my child's genius.*

Many parents feel that they are unable to support their child's education because they were not very good at mathematics and/or English. Let's destroy this negative belief with a few words. I CAN ACHIEVE! Once this has become your daily mantra look at all the things in your life you have been successful at, and all your skills and see how these successes and skills can transfer into being a good parent-teacher. E.g., are you patient? Do you have good organisational skills? Are you sociable? Are you inquisitive? This positive reassessment will make you feel more confident in taking on the task of being a parent-teacher.

Children and Mathematics: the stages

➢ Children need to be introduced to mathematics through activities like pairing, matching, sorting, pairing and ordering.
➢ The next stage is counting.
➢ Dot-to-dot drawing number work is useful
➢ Reading numerals and linking numerals with counting
➢ Counting and comparing
➢ Introduce your child to the + , -, x ? signs plus the 0 sign
➢ This stage is followed by the four operations of addition, subtraction multiplication (learning tables) and division.
➢ Introduce your child to measures, shape and space. Investigate plane shapes first; measure with familiar objects, hands etc.
➢ Place value.

- ➤ Fractions
- ➤ Handling data

The Stages in Your Child's Mathematical Skills: A Further Investigation

Pamela Liebeck, in her book, *How Children Learn Mathematics*, points out that children's mathematical experience progresses through a sequence of abstraction which can be categorised as:

E - experience with physical objects
L - spoken language that describes the experience
P - pictures that represent the experience
S - written symbols that generalises the experience

This model will allow the parent-teacher to observe more carefully their child's play, and more importantly to set exercises for their child to undertake. You should also record how they have performed these exercises.

Your Child's Mathematical Record Sheet

	Observation Notes	Future Strategy
Experience with physical objects	E.g., recognises and names shapes. Able to sort and order selected objects.	E.g., set tasks to encourage estimation of objects.
Mathematical language development	E.g., uses mathematical language , for example, count on, one less, number before.	E.g., encourage child to choose numbers for problems and to make up their own story problems.
Visual experience & understanding of the tasks	E.g., uses language confidently to describe position and compare.	E.g., set tasks which show mathematical problems of increasing complexity.
Their understanding of mathematical symbols	E.g., recognises addition and subtraction signs.	E.g., use symbols in different contexts.

Visualise your child succeeding in all of their activities. Encourage them to estimate heights, lengths and when you are shopping give them tasks to calculate say the cost of certain items etc. Introduce them to the language of mathematics by letting them hear you use phrases like:

This is bigger than...
This is longer than...
This weighs more than...
This is in groups of...
These match...

This has a bigger area...
This container holds more than...

Mathematics literacy is very important and so is your child's ability to estimate. By visualising mathematical operations and bringing mathematics into their everyday life experience the child feels less

A few months ago I attended a numeracy course, and I happened to sit next to another teacher who was clearly the best student in the class. She was a Nigerian lady and seemed to have a pleasant smile on her face as she did her work. She would always finish her work first, and sit there with quiet confidence. After a few weeks of this I asked her how she had developed her mathematical skills. She informed me that when she was a child, her mother used to send her to the market in Nigeria to buy groceries for the home. She would be given a small budget, and when she arrived at the market she would bargain with the people selling produce in the market. She said she was constantly having to do calculations in her head to see how much she could get for her money, whilst also having to outsmart the marketeers. It was here that her skills in mathematics were developed.

Mathematics is about visualisation which is part of estimation. The child needs to be made aware that mathematics can be fun and mathematics is all around us. (Refer to first section to review what maths skills your child should have in whichever year they are in). You should look at books on art and mathematics, stories on mathematics and even read books on the history of mathematics which is a very

interesting and important subject.

How Your Child Learns

Learning involves four processes:

- intake of information
- retention of information
- recall of information
- application of information

This model assumes that your child is a bit like a computer. As parent-teachers you need to go beyond this and consider how culture shapes the learning process, and probe into the wisdom already existing within the child. The role of the Parent-teacher is to encourage creative thinking. The child should therefore be shown skills, strategies and learning techniques.

Useful teaching styles:

- Identify the skill and explain to your child.
- Demonstrate the skill
- Allow your child to practice the learnt skill

- Remember to help your child to recap and review their completed work

The most important thing to develop in teaching your child how to learn is for you to develop a *narrative of enquiry*, that is, you should encourage your child to learn by taking every opportunity to investigate the world they live in. Sentences beginning with who, why and when, and addressed to your child simply makes them observe and question the world they live in. This is important as much of the educational literature being produced is mechanical; doesn't encourage enquiry and the child is simply fed work and information that has little relevance to their world.

Teaching your child to read or improve your child's reading

- Use both phonemes (sounds) and sight reading but don't overly rely on the latter unless your child shows a strong preference for this style.
- Read to your child regularly and have them read to you.
- Discuss what you have read together.
- Keep a spelling/vocabulary book.
- Create word games e.g., write a simple poem about a favourite relative, or pet. Perhaps provide your child with key words.

Improve your child's reading

In her book, *'Why Children Can't Read'* Diane McGinness writes: '..to learn an alphabet writing system, a child must be taught the sounds in words....the next step is to teach children how each of these sounds is spelled in a carefully sequenced way'.

This section of the book deals with reading because I have found that children of all ages still have not been taught sufficient reading strategies.

Educators will normally tell you that there are two methods to teach your child to read; the phonics method and the whole language method. There is in fact a third method which uses phonemes.

- Phonics teaches a child to read using sounds of the alphabet.
- Whole language (whole words) teaches a child to read using recognition of whole words through memory and context etc.
- Phonemes teaches your child to read using the sounds of the words and it is this method that the author prefers and sees as being the most effective.

How Your Child Reads

A child learns to read primarily through hearing. This might sound silly, as most people think that they learn to read by primarily using their eyes. A child has to first hear the sounds of the language. So let's note a few key points:

- A letter or a combination of letters (digraphs) is a symbol for a sound.

- Letters combine to make sounds of the English language

- The English language has basic sounds which should be taught to your child.

Diane McGuinness identifies four main skill areas for five year olds: awareness of phonemes and sequence of phonemes in words; the logic of the alphabet code; fine motor control and visual scanning and analysis of visual detail. These are often lacking in the 7 - 8 year old and a quick revision programme can help a great deal. These skills are useful for children of all ages if they haven't acquired these skills.

Revision Reading Skills programme for the child, regardless of age, who still has difficulty.

Sounds of the alphabet

Read to your child and discuss what has been read.

- Teach first sounds: cat, cap, cut

- Teach last sounds: bat, hat, cat

- Teach middle sounds: big, hug, sat

The logic of the alphabet system

Fine Motor Control

Give your child dot-to-dot exercises. Let them copy and trace letter shapes. Encourage them to say the sounds as they write the letters.

Visual Discrimination and Scanning

By encouraging the child to copy and say the sounds this will help them to look at words and 'see' the sounds.

Useful tips on Reading

- Read to your child for 15 minutes every day.
- Use more than one reading scheme to add variety and guard against them memorising words rather than understanding the sounds.
- It's okay for your child to learn a few sight words when they are reading a book in order to aid general understanding and enjoyment.
- Use a pen or your finger to guide the reading as this helps with tracking and can speed up the slow reader.
- Discuss the book that is to be read. Name the author and illustrator, and read the blurb at the back of the book.
- Discuss what has been read to check for understanding.

Exploring Sounds

Speech is made by sounds the mouth make. Make your child aware by saying these sounds to them and make them repeat them after you. You are trying to get them to become aware of the movements of their mouth as it makes a sound.

Ask them where does the tongue go when you say these sounds (letters) to develop their speech awareness and control.

Sounds	Movement of lips and tongue- notes
a	
b	
d	
th	
ch	

Step 1

Parent-Teacher instruction:
- first introduce these sounds to your child
- Vowels make the long sounds (a e i o u)
- Consonants make the short sounds

Vowel Sound	Key word	Alphabet letter
a	sat	a
e	set	e
i	sit	i
o	dog	o
u	hut	u

Step 2

Now let us select a few sounds (letters) to teach your child to hear.

a	as in ant	e	as in eat	I	as in
b	as in ball	f	as in fat	j	as in jug
c	as in cat	g	as in got	k	as in kit
d	as in dad	h	as in hat	l	as in lip

Step 3

Now encourage your child to make these sounds, focusing on the end sound.

bed	sad	bag	was	sat	dry
rat	pin	nut	him	kid	hop
few	key	fox	pip	lad	gas

Step 4

Now make your child say the middle sound and then make them write the middle letter in the space provided.

bed	sad	bag	was	sat	dry
rat	pin	nut	him	kid	hop
few	key	fox	pip	lad	gas

Spelling Patterns for Your Child

Here are some exercises for your child.

1. Make these letters (sounds) into whole words.
2. Write a sentence using one word from each pattern.
3. Say the word aloud as you write it.

a) E.g. shop   sh   sh   sh

....

b) E.g. blow   bl   bl   bl

....

c) E.g. clip   cl   cl   cl
....

d) E.g. flat   fl   fl   fl

....

e) E.g. glad   gl   gl   gl

....

f) E.g. play   pl   pl   pl

....

g) E.g. slap   sl   sl   sl

....

h) E.g. brag   br   br   br

....

i) E.g. from   fr   fr   fr

....

j) E.g. small   sm   sm   sm

....

k) E.g. stop   st   st   st

....

l) E.g. what   wh   wh   wh

Double vowel sounds

Say the sounds aloud and then write a sentence with the word containing the oo sound in it.

Say oo   as in look

_____

Say oa   as in boat

_____

Say ee   as in seek

_____

Say ea   as in seat

_____

Word Endings

bal	as in tribal
bel	as in label
ble	as in bible, bubble, scribble and table
cal	as in magical
cle	as in uncle
ckle	as in pickle, trickle and tackle
dal	as in medal and bridal
dle	as in candle, fiddle and middle
fle	as in shuffle and sniffle
ful	as in awful, beautiful, careful and grateful
gle	as in eagle, struggle and wiggle

Sight words

Sight words are words that have irregular spellings so they have to be memorised 'by sight'.

In 'Why Children Can't Read', Diane McGuinness identifies 37 sight words that need to be memorised by the child. Make your child copy these words:

a	could	do	does	door
enough	father	friend	give	gone
great	have	into	live	of
once	one	people	said	says
should	the	their	there	through
to	together	today	two	very
was	were	what	where	who
would				

Below is a useful summary chart of the various reading goals your child should achieve. I've based this summary on the work of Carmen and Geoffrey McGuiness from their book *Reading Reflex* (1998).

- 10 Years - Read one fiction and non-fiction book per month. Read two magazines per month.
- 9 Years - Reads three and two syllable words accurately. Read one fiction and non-fiction book per month. Read one appropriate magazine per month.
- 8 Years - Reads two syllable words with accuracy. Read single syllable words accurately. Read one fiction and non-fiction book per month. Read two to three short books per week. Read one appropriate magazine.
- 7 Years - Reads single syllable words accurately. Reads most single syllable words accurately. Reads most two syllable words accurately. Spells most single syllable words. Reads one to two books to parents each week.
- 6 Years - Reads most single syllable words. Spells single syllable words fairly well. Reads to parents each day between 10 to 15 minutes.
- 5 Years - Can read any three sound word. Beginning to read more complex words containing consonants.
- 4 Years - Beginning to read and spell three-sound words accurately.

Dealing with dyslexia

The word 'dyslexia' comes from the Greek (dys lexikos) which means 'difficulty with words or language'. Our working definition of dyslexia should therefore be a child who has difficulty with learning to read and write, in particular in learning to spell and in expressing their thoughts. It is estimated that 10% of children in the Western World have dyslexia. Some research shows that boys are more likely to have dyslexia by approximately 5 to 1, however not all experts agree with this.

What Causes Dyslexia?

There are a number of theories as to what causes dyslexia, some experts believe that dyslexia is due to lesions in the brain; that it is genetic, and some experts say that dyslexia does not exist; that it is simply a reading and specific learning disability. So, this reading disability, might be due to the child having been taught to read incorrectly.

How to Recognise if Your Child Has Dyslexia

The signs that a child has dyslexia may be:

- Reads slowly and hesitates.
- Moves head when reading.
- Uses their finger to follow the text.
- Loses where they are and misses out large chunks of the text.
- Misreads familiar words and misses out lines of the text.

- Stresses the wrong syllable.
- Misreads words that look similar.
- Reads the same word twice.
- Writes letters in the wrong order.
- Can't write letters when they are told the name of the letters.
- Can't match sounds.
- Ignores punctuation.
- Make up words that have no meaning.

What Parents Can Do If Their Child Is Diagnosed Dyslexic

- Encourage and motivate the child to feel positive about specialist support.
- Liase with the specialist (and main teacher) and get yourself trained to take a leading role in the remediating process.
- The specialist will probably put the child on a spelling and reading programme. Provide what help you can in supporting this.
- Don't lose your temper if the child shows slow progress. Be patient!
- Join a dyslexic support group.
- Help them with their homework or get what help you can from other sources.
- Engage them in relaxation techniques such as visualisation, yoga etc.
- Use varied learning styles to help support the child.
- Computers can often give the dyslexic child a great deal of confidence and support.

The anguish, frustration and stress that the dyslexic pupil experiences is often underestimated and misunderstood. Over the years I have worked with both adults and children who have dyslexia and based on these experiences I now present a fictitious letter that might have been written by any of the adults as they reflect on their schooling. I hope that this letter gives you a greater understanding of the frustration of someone who has a reading disability.

Dear Mr Barnes,

Micky Dillon here. Reckon you don't remember me. The ginger haired kid that used to sit at the back. I was in 11 G. Left in '94. The year someone tried to burn down the bike shed. Swear it wasn't me. Anyway, I heard you were retiring, so I reckon I'd drop you a line to say thanks and stuff. Thanks for helping me with me dyslexia. Untill you came it was hell. Kept playing truant 'cause I hated school. Teachers hated me too. I'd get into fights so I could get excluded, so I didn't have to do work. You were the first one who worked me out. You see we never had words in my family, not intellectual words. Don't get me wrong, we had plenty of love and that, especially when Uncle Benjamin sang and played the piano down the pub, but I wanted words to get me out this kind of prison me head was in. Words just kept deserting me, especially when me mum died, and I wanted to write something to put in her grave. But I couldn't. The words wouldn't come.

But anyway, as I was saying, you worked me out. At first, when me dad got your letter about dyslexia he fought I'd done something wrong so he clipped me round the head. He didn't know what dyslexia meant. Nor did I. Leroy down the market told him. Anyhow, you got me in your class and kept making me say these sounds of letters. After a while I started to hear the words. I kept going to your session, even though the other kids kept calling me a sissy. Never forgot what you taught me.

A few years ago when me little girl started school, she came back with a reading book. I was supposed to read to her. I was scared that I wouldn't read it properly, and I was scared that she'd have this dyslexia thing like me. Scared stiff I was. But I started to read. Was one of the greatest moments of me life. Next fing I know I'm reading every bleeding thing I can get me hands on. Romantic novels, history books, autobiographies and even poetry. That's right Dylan Thomas poetry. He was a screwed up bastard! A few months later I've only gone and landed a job selling encyclopaedias. So all those words I couldn't read I'm selling them now and making a tidy few bob at that! Anyway, just wanted to say thanks. Wanted to wish you well in your retirement. Also, just wanted to tell you that it was me that set fire to the shed. Sorry.

Good luck mate.

Micky (From 11 G)

Attention Deficit Hyperactivity Disorder (ADHD)

Attention Deficit Hyperactivity Disorder describes a behaviour in children that can see them inattentive, distractable, impulsive and hyperactive. These children might live in their own world where they don't hear what is said to them, or they can be so distracted they cannot focus on anything for any length of time. They might often act without any thought, which in a classroom situation can get them into trouble. They can often be disruptive, fidgety and in constant motion. Some 'experts' believe that ADHD is a genetic disorder, others that it is a disorder caused by diet or environment. However, ADHD affects many children. In England it is estimated that 5 per cent of children have ADHD. This is a very large figure and we must wonder if attentional control in children might also be due to other factors, thereby making ADHD a symptom rather than a cause.

Dianne McGuinness interestingly identifies the two operational systems in the brain of a child. These brain systems control distractibility and attention span. She points out that distractibility has a purpose. When everything is new the brain of the child has to code everything important into memory. Of course children vary in the extent of this distractibility. My own experience, whilst I admit that I have come across children who do appear to have a condition that matches ADHD only rarely, is that by far the most prevalent cause has been boredom whereby the child is totally disengaged from school. Dianne McGuinness, in *Why Children Can't Read,* writes (p184):

> Because teachers are never provided with training and skills to teach reading correctly, their classrooms are filling up with children who are 'dyslexic', 'can't pay attention', or who 'aren't', or 'have emotional problems'. We are blaming the victims because teachers aren't properly trained to do their job.

Again, as a result of running Ebony Education we have seen dozens of children brought to us with school reports that have branded them as having poor attention spans which have partially misled the parents. Many children find the school experience alienating, even those who appear to have no attention or hyperactive issues. Many children and teachers find the curriculum restrictive and unimaginative. It is the school (often the reluctant teacher) that has to deliver this curriculum. Children who don't respond to this delivery are labelled. When race, class and learning difficulty also become factors then the education system blames the child, the family of the child, or the community from which the children come from. The child wants a school experience that is meaningful. As a result the child is demotivated, uninspired and confused. If reading problems are also a factor, then they will not be attentive because they know the teacher sees them as a problem, and the learning task that involves reading makes them want to engage in another activity. The teaching profession does not openly challenge the effectiveness of its professional practice. So, in talking about ADHD we are not talking about as many cases as is being claimed.

Diagnosing ADHD

In Learning and Attention Disorders, Dr William Feldman identifies simple steps, which a specialist will go through in diagnosing ADHD.

1. Identify the symptoms (impulsiveness, hyperactivity).
2. Establish when the symptoms first appeared.
3. State where the symptoms occur (school etc).
4. Assess how severe the symptoms are. That is, is there clear evidence that the condition is making the child disfunctional at school or home.
5. Rule out other possible conditions/causes for the behaviour.

Once the diagnosis has been completed then the specialist will advise on a course of action. The issue might be whether the child should be prescribed medication or not. Again the parents should get as much information and qualified advice as possible.

Further research for the parent-teacher

Conduct further basic research (summary notes) into:

Teaching a child mathematics
- Teaching a child how to read
- Dyslexia, reading disability and ADHD

A Poetical Gift to You From the Tree

Modern storyteller weave the tale,
For the future labour of the children

Are you the clown of words,
Bringing puzzles for our children,
That they may piece together
Forbidden solutions of debt, poverty and war?

Modern storyteller weave a tale
The future child sits by your night fire.

Sit under our Tree,
Let the small ones juggle with your words,
So they may document our tragedy
And save those that suckle for dear life.

Modern storyteller weave a story
That has a happy ending for the few survivors.

Stage 4 - Creative Learning: mind maps and music for your child

Key words: visualisation, music, poetry, art, joy & harmony

Aims
- To introduce the parent teacher to the practice of visualising to achieve goals.
- To introduce the parent-teacher to art as a way of releasing their child's hidden talents.
- To introduce the parent-teacher to the developmental stages in their child's artistic skills.
- To introduce the parent-teacher to the art of story telling.

African Proverb
*If you think education is expensive,
try ignorance*
            Uganda

To visualise means that you imagine yourself doing something or an experience, and make this imagining as real as possible by experiencing the smells, noise and sights of the imagined event and situation. You need to visualise yourself successfully supporting and taking charge of your child's education. Draw pictures or write poems of this happening. When you visualise this happening see yourself using this book, taking your child to the library, using computer packages on the PC. Be precise. Energy follows attention. You are programming your subconscious, and this subconscious will become active in making you more aware of the whole process of holistic education.

Mind Maps and creativity

The Brain

The brain weighs more than three pounds and uses lots of oxygen. It has over one trillion neurons and is located in the head. The cell body of the neuron has a nucleus and it is here that the DNA is contained. The DNA is a code which has information about us. Neurons communicate with one another, and the more stimulation your child receives the greater this communication which develops new pathways that helps the child to remember. For the purposes of studying how the brain operates we can look at two models that will give us insight into how the brain works and how best we can develop our teaching and the child's learning.

The Triune Brain Model

Dr. Paul MacLean (1990) developed the model of the triune brain. MacLean said that the human brain went through three evolutionary stages. The first part of the brain to evolve was the reptillian brain. This part of the brain controls the heart rate, the blood pressure, the digestive system and additional voluntary functions. Also, this part of the brain is instinctual and territorial. In learning a child will often mark out their territory and feel upset if someone invades this territory whether it is physical or emotional. The paleomammalian brain was the second part of the brain to emerge according to MacLean. This mammalian part of the brain emerged with mammals. Located here are emotion, nurturing and curiosity brain functions, and all facilities for holding a mammalian group together. The neocortex is the newest part of the brain to evolve, where brain functions like language manipulation, problem solving and self-awareness all occur. These functions allow us to learn from experience and to intervene when we experience instinctive feelings of say anger and fear. However, when we are angry or fearful we switch to the animal/reptillian behaviour which creates a negative learning state. It is therefore desirable that the pupil and parent have strategies for addressing this. Later in the book we will see just such strategies such as positive visualisation, breathing techniques, self-observation and affirmations.

Right Hemisphere Left Hemisphere Model

In this model the brain is said to have two hemispheres and each hemisphere of the brain has its own way of knowing and perceiving, but they can, and do, work together (although one half might take a more leading role depending on what activity the brain is engaged with). In drawing it is thought that the right brain dominates as this half of the brain is involved in visual processing. It is the right hemisphere where creativity takes place, using imagination, intuition, rhythm and colour. Ideally you should aim to develop both sides of your child's brain. The left and right hemispheres of the brain are in charge of the following areas:

The Left Hemisphere

Logic
Sequence
Reason
Orders
Separate

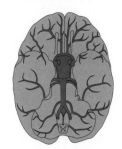

The Right Hemisphere:

Imaginative
Creative
Holistic
Colours
Pictures

The brain has millions of neurons which must be kept active, must be stimulated and nourished through good diet and activity. At any one time the brain has millions of chemical reactions taking place. We can stimulate our child's brain through:

Creative Play
A variety of toys
Reading
Movement and learning exercises
Listening and playing music
Mind Games like chess and dominoes
Breathing exercises

Our brains, though capable of linear thinking, perform more creatively when they think in an associating way. That is, a central idea may have associating ideas which allow for the creative exploration of the central topic. By noting this, a system of note-taking/note-making can be devised. Such a system has been devised by Tony Buzan and is called Mind Mapping.

What are mind maps?

Mind Mapping is a visual note-taking/note-making system that is an excellent tool for creative thinking as it allows for a lot of information to be structured on a mind map using simple rules. And these rules allow us to remember things easily. One of these rules is to use key words. Key words are words that incorporate what is desired to be learnt and allow for quick recall. The use of key words in mind mapping is based on the fact that our mind does not necessarily recall in sentences but in key words and images, so mind mapping also uses images. The mind maps will also help you to develop your creativity and organisational skills.

Mind Maps Use:

➢ Pictures/images

➢ Colour (people are 80% more likely to read something if it's in colour)
➢ Key words
➢ Associations
➢ Dimensions
➢ Humour

The Mind Map speaks to both the left and right side of the brain.

Mind Maps can be used for a number of things like:

➢ Creative Thinking
➢ Note-taking
➢ Team meetings
➢ Creative writing
➢ Planning

Here is how you Mind Map

- Get a piece of paper and lay it out horizontally.
- Get some coloured pencils.
- In the centre of the paper draw your central image i.e., the topic about which your mind map is about.
- Use several colours in drawing your central image.
- With each new idea draw a thick curved branch.
- On each branch write in capitals a key word.
- Additional ideas should also have a branch that is less thick.
- Use as many images as possible.
- Use dimension.

NB: You should always read a mind map from the centre, then look at its branches.

Now you have a go! Make a mind map on your child's education.

The Art of Discovery

One of the great benefits of fine art is that it teaches the child to see. Art is not simply about drawing well (although that is one of the obvious benefits), it is about seeing with fresh eyes; seeing without prejudice or bias. Out of all the subjects we have offered over the last 17 years, fine art has been the one that has captivated the minds of the children the most. What's more, I'm not a fine art teacher, yet, through imaginative lesson planning I have used art to open the minds of children; to help them explore topics such as being a victim of bullying; representation, the environment, racism, disability and youth culture.

Stages in a child's art development:

1   10 months to two-and-a-half year old - scribble-art
2   Two-and-a-half years to four years - scribble symbols now begin to

represent something in the child's reality.

3   Four to eight years picture stories with increasing detail
4   Nine years plus greater realism is attempted.
5   At around 11 years art-illiteracy often sets in if the child is not stimulated.

Art and design is a visual language that allows the child to communicate using shape, colour, line, form etc. The well structured artistic experience can develop your child's visual vocabulary, allowing them to further explore their culture and that of other people; also, it can allow them to explore themselves and their world. Although I now present a simple step by step programme to develop your child's artistic abilities you can attempt the stages simultaneously, sequentially, or improvise etc.

2-Dimensional Visual Language

Resources
Pencils, coloured pencils, cartridge paper, tracing paper, charcoal, newsprint, pastels, crayons, water & colours.

Tasks
1. Draw, copy and/or trace simple images.
2. Cut out pictures.
3. Colour in drawn pictures.
4. Finger painting.
5. Make collages.

Make the child aware from as young an age as possible of positive representation. A black child will often colour a self portrait or portrait of family members green or blue. They should be encouraged to colour people of colour in the appropriate shades of brown. The children's book, *When I Look in the Mirror* by Sopoeia Greywolf, is a good text to help address this issue.

3-Dimensional Visual Language

1. Modelling simple shapes with plasticine.
2. Cutting and shaping.
3. The use of textiles.

Formally experiment with colour
The primary colours are red, blue and yellow. Pictures and objects can be painted with these colours before introducing secondary colours. Secondary colours are formed by mixing two primary colours, e.g;

Red + blue = violet

Blue + yellow = green

Red + yellow = orange

Your task is to simply encourage your child to experiment and enjoy making marks, marks that with careful thought can mean and represent so much. You might wish to play music as your child paints or draws.

Photography

There are many branches of photography (photo-journalism, fashion, landscape, portraiture etc) which serve various functions but they all require the person behind the camera to see. For children, a camera like polaroid, or even a disposable one which gives quick results can encourage them to observe the world they live in more closely.

Set your child simple and agreed tasks like taking photographs of family and friends; documenting social occasions, taking photographs of nature around them. It is also important for your child to be encouraged to catalogue the pictures in albums and build up their small photographic library. When anyone starts photography they normally take the obvious tourist type picture, that is, they stand and take shots of the person's full length. As your child gets more adept at photography, encourage them to experiment by taking close up shots; shots from different angles, and make them study their results. By studying their results they will be more aware of what type of photograph they are taking and therefore look more carefully at the subject.

Three photographers whose work you might wish to look at for inspiration are W. Eugene Smith, Gordon Parks and Eve Arnold.

Creative Therapy

Do not underestimate how art can be used to unlock your child's genius. When I first started Ebony we only provided small group tuition in English and mathematics, but it was after a few months that we could see that the children needed more than this. Some seemed shy, uncommunicative and others seemed not to know much about the world they were living in and their cultural history. There were other issues, such as dealing with bullying, racism and peer pressure, so I soon realised that we needed another subject and one that could incorporate a number of themes, issues and teaching styles.

In 1988 we started our creative studies programme that looked at the above issues and more, and also used the arts as a teaching and perhaps even a therapeutic resource. However, I hadn't realised the true potential of this creative studies until the teacher who had been teaching this subject was absent and I had to cover this particular class. I had not long given a workshop on the Harlem Renaissance, an African-American arts movement around 1925-1935 (dates differ). As this was fresh in my mind, I walked into the class and told the children they were going to make their own cultural archives, and investigate what these African-American artists had done, and why they had done what they did. I was a little apprehensive, perhaps thinking that the subject might be a little grown up for the children, but it was a lesson in never underestimating children's ability to learn as long as the topic is made interesting and accessible. I brought in poems by Claude

Mckay, novels by Zora Neal Hurston, photographic books by the photographer James Van Der Zee, and pictures of other leading Harlem Renaissance figures like W.E.B Dubois, Marcus Garvey and the filmmaker Oscar Micheaux. I simply came into the hall with as much materials as I could find, and more importantly with early Jazz music, which to me simply conveyed the mood of the times.

The children sat in a big circle. We did our usual warm up exercises using yoga to focus on balance, spinning and stretching, and with me prompting them to perform 'Creative Burst' exercises where the children would burst out laughing, crying and cheering; an exercise that helps rid them of their inhibitions. They had to look at pictures of artists of the times and just talk about what these artists were trying to do regarding representation and the black experience in segregated America. Within a matter of minutes, the children were drawing, cutting and pasting; trying to draw and celebrate themselves, using graphics, experimenting with colours. The class was quiet yet busy with work and creativity. It taught me about spontaneous teaching; about letting excitement quicken the pace of the lesson, and never underestimating what a child is capable of learning as long as it has value to their lives.

The Harmony of Childhood

As hearing takes place in the inner ear where the auditory nerve cells are located, the musical experience stimulates brain cell activity.
Research indicates that certain types of music: aids learning, improves mathematical skills, problem-solving, concentration, reading ability, language development, listening skills, self-esteem and promotes self-discipline in children. It is therefore advisable that the parent-teacher should encourage their child to learn to play a musical instrument and/or engage in some kind of musical activity. You might wish to play music as background music occasionally when your child is studying, or as a musical exercise, whereby the child has to deliberately listen to the various instruments, or simply play music to relax and stimulate the child.

Music to Remember

Music that has 60 beats per minute helps with memory as this has frequencies which in turn helps harmonising brain waves. This helps create the ideal learning state which Dilip Mukerajea in *Superbrain* (1996) calls, relaxed alertness. Music by the composers Bach and Vivaldi that fall into this 60 beat per minute category are ideal. In addition, faster tempo music by Mozart, Beethoven and Brahms can further stimulate the brain. Jazz music can also be used and the music of Duke Ellington should be considered.

Composer	Title of Music
Johann Sebastian Bach (1685 - 1750)	• Arioso • Largo from Harpsichord Con in C Major
Antonio Lucio Vivaldi (1678 - 1741)	• Largo from "Winter" from The Four Seasons • Largo from Concerto in D major for

	Guitar and Strings
Duke Ellington (1899 - 1974)	• Mood Indigo • Warm Valley

The Power of the Story

The power of the story and how the story can be used as an educational tool cannot be underestimated. Below is the first chapter of a short children's novel. The aim of the story is to raise awareness about autism and learning disability; introduce you to the world of the animated universe as seen through the eyes of children, and raise your awareness regarding environmental issues. Following this we'll look at how you can develop your own story writing skills to help unlock your child's genius, so let's begin with a story of a little girl.

A Story by a Little Girl - The Learning Tree

...It all started on the Friday. Friday is special. She told us so. I mean old Mrs Patridge. She's our next door neighbour. She would go to one of her small statues in the garden and say a little prayer. She's mad you know. Since Mr Partridge died whilst digging a pond in the garden, she just stays in the house and sometimes cries, and sometimes laughs. A big nut-case Dad says. But on Friday the moon always shines on the old statue. So it had to be Friday. That's when she came. My little brother and sister were being real naughty. Cleopatra, my sister, wouldn't let mum braid her hair. Mum was vexed. And Kobi, my brother kept getting in trouble for climbing the old apple tree in the garden. Perhaps it wasn't their fault. We all seemed to know that our summer holidays were going to be special. A few weeks before, our grandma arrived. Grandma came with really big suitcases full of rum, nutmeg and bush-tea. In fact it was Grandma, as she was plaiting her wiry grey hair, that told us that something wonderful was going to happen. She laughed. "Just watch dat tree. It full of mischief, she said. So each day, before and after breakfast we would keep watching the tree. We'd take turns but Kobi would fall asleep. It was a Friday, that the old dirty van pulled up in front of the house next door. Cleopatra spotted it first. She screamed, and shouted. Toby and I raced down the stairs. Kobi fell. I picked him up. I then fell, and he picked me up. When we peeped through the netting, we saw two big men. They swore, stretched and scratched before kicking open the front gate and walked through the tangly weeds lining the footpath. At first we watched them take out tables, chairs, beds and black bags, then we got hungry so Cleopatra made some peanut butter sandwiches, and we kept watching through the netted curtains. Everything we saw made us worried. Imitation antique is what Cleopatra said. But as the lazy evening came, the men emerged from the house, wiped sweat from their brows and drove off in the big van that puffed out smoke as it went. Suddenly we were disappointed. All that was left was furniture. The house next door was still empty.

Shadows took over the garden. Grandma's moon was coming out. We all began to get disappointed, and a little sad but Grandma cheered us up with fresh roast corn. Suddenly, Kobi, who had been looking out of the window, started shouting. "Look", he said, jumping all over the sofa. "It's them!" Well me and Cleopatra raced down the stairs, threw back the curtains and saw this slim woman with bags, get out of the car. She seemed to stop, look around, almost as if she was checking out the area. Then, she appeared to be waiting for someone. She looked like a teacher, but she was too groomed for a teacher. Suddenly, the back door of the car opened and out came the strangest little girl you ever saw. She had big floppy plaits, a sad mouth and wonderful eyes that looked as if they had only recently discovered the world. She could only have been nine or so, but the way she held the ladies hands it seemed that she was three. Again the two of them looked at the house. They turned and looked at us but we ducked. When we popped our heads out again they were gone. "Where've they gone?" asked Cleopatra, as if it had somehow been my fault that they had disappeared. For a few seconds no one knew what to do. Grandma, who heard our rantings from upstairs, came down with her slippers, sipping her herb tea, and with her usual chuckle said: "Go round de back. Me sure you can glimpse dem some more." As usual Grandma was right. We raced round the back, half knocking over mum who yelled at us to get inside before it got dark.

  We sat under the apple tree. The stars were big. One of them kept winking at us. Cleopatra asked the moon who the new neighbours were, but the moon kept quiet. Everything was a secret. And even Quietness came and started playing in the garden with the breeze. Then, as the need for sleep started to make Kobi restless, the back door opened, and we saw the same head of plaits come out into the garden. It was the little girl. Her steps were full of discovery. Her finger tips seemed to touch the evening air, feeling secrets that Mrs Partridge had left. Cleopatra prodded me. She always does that when she's scared. I poked my head out over the garden fence and said," Hello, I'm Dominique." The little girl got scared. She put her hands over her eyes. Her light white dress began to shiver. Cleopatra and Kobi ran up alongside me. "I'm Cleopatra". "I'm Kobi; I come in peace. I come only to defeat evil," said Kobi who was still caught up in his Star Wars game. But her face was full of fingers. Finally, after we just stood there smiling the best we could, the fingers parted. Her big eyes looked at us. Slowly her mouth opened but no words came. Her mouth opened again, but again no words came. Finally, she tried again, and this time a little squeaky voice was heard. "I'm Shola". She was about to run back inside, but her mother came out. She looked as if she'd had a long day. She was tall and beautiful, just like the models in the magazines. "Hello", she said. "I see you've met Shola". "Oh yes," I replied, trying to be friendly. The mother, took Shola by the shoulders and encouraged her to come a little closer to us. "She's perfectly okay, but she's just a little different that's all". "Different I said?" "Yes," replied the mother. "She's autistic". Cleopatra, who always thinks she knows everything stepped forward and said, "We're English but our parents come from the Caribbean. Where's Autisticland?" The lady laughed. I cringed. "No, autism is a learning disability. She doesn't communicate quite like you but she's just as human as you are". We all smiled not quite sure what she was saying. "It's late. I'm Ngozi. I think I better get her to bed. It's been a long day. Night, night." Shola gave us a little wave. We stood under the apple tree, still mesmerised by the little girl.

  An hour later we were all in bed. Kobi was snoring. Cleopatra was fast asleep, but I kept looking out the window at the apple tree, wondering about Shola and her autism. I kept wanting to help her. I knew that this was going to be the start of the great adventure that Grandma had told us about. But then sleep came.

The next morning, after horrible porridge that Mum said would make us healthy, me and Cleopatra went on the internet, whilst Kobi played with his Star Wars game and kept watch to see if Shola would come out into the garden again. It was a hot day. A Saturday. We downloaded as much as we could find and as much as we could read about autism. There were a lot of big words. It seemed like autism was a lot of different things. Anyway, after all the reading, we knocked on Grandma's door. It took a long time for her to open it. This time Grandma wasn't like she normally was. She had her head wrapped in white cloth. Beads were hanging from her neck. Incense made Kobi sneeze. Grandma was different. "Come in," she said opening the door. "Now, what can I do for you?" "Well Grandma, we've got a new neighbour. She's a little girl." "And she's auto," shouted out Kobi, unable to hold back. "He means autistic," Cleopatra corrected. "And what do you want from me," Grandma asked. I took a deep breath. "Well, we thought you could give us some of your herb tea to make her better. Make her speak properly". Grandma looked serious, as if I'd said something wrong. "Well," she started, looking over at her jars of herbs as if they were people, "I can give you something to speak to her with. It might not be what you expect, but it will allow you to be able to talk to her." Grandma gave us some herbs in a brown paper bag and showed us the door.

　　　We knew that we couldn't make it whilst Mum and Dad were around. We also knew that they had to go to a big meeting at the town hall about some big new development happening in the area. So we waited for them to leave, and that evening we boiled some water, poured it in the cup where we had put the herb tea and waited for magic to brew. After a while the steam stopped coming out of the cup. We walked out in to the back garden and sat under the apple tree, hoping that Shola would again come out in the garden. Perhaps god heard our little prayers, because not long afterwards she came. She had a light blue dress on this time. Her plaits were a lot more tame. "Shola," called Cleopatra in a whisper, hoping not to wake Grandma who was supposed to be looking after us.

　　　This time Shola wasn't scared. She came over to us. Before we knew what was happening she had hitched her dress, climbed over our broken fence and stood before us. We thought that we now had her trust, but she walked straight past us, to the apple tree where she seemed to be talking to someone or something, but we could see no one. Suddenly she started dancing, singing and twirling around, almost like she was drunk with happiness on seeing old friends. "Shola," I called. "We've got some herb tea. It can help you. It can stop you being autistic. Just drink it." At that moment, Grandma, still wearing her white head wrap and beads, came out from nowhere. "No children, de herb tea is not for Shola. It's for you." "Us?" replied Cleopatra. "We can talk properly." Grandma laughed. "Can you? Can you talk to the plants, the moon, the flowers, the animals, the leprechauns, and all the other little people that live in the tree. No you can't." Grandma took the cup of herb tea from my hand, put it to my lips and told me to take a sip. I took one, then Cleopatra took another and finally Kobi took a sip. Suddenly the apple tree grew big. Little people began to poke their heads out of the leaves of the tree. And Shola spoke to us in quite plain English. "Come with me, please come and I'll show you a wonderful world. But we need your help, for all the trees of the world are dying. We need you to help save the world. Please come." Shola stretched out her hand and the great adventure that Grandma had talked about began.

The End...for now

Little stories like this one can often further demonstrate inclusiveness to learners who have a disability or learning difficulty.

Story Writing

We have already looked at basic story writing but now, as we recognise the importance of story writing as a teaching and learning tool, we might look to further develop our skills in good characterisation. When developing a character you should complete a character profile which will help you build a character that is believable. A character profile will consist of:

- Name and age of character
- Appearance of character
- Main events of character's childhood

- Characters likes and dislikes
- Character's ambitions
- Character's main relationships

By answering the above you will have developed a well thought out character.
    When your child reads a book or if you have to read with them, it is always good to analyse the characters as this helps in understanding the story. The character profile can be adapted and therefore help you in posing questions to your child when asking them about the characters in the book. For example, you might ask your child to describe the character's personality, or their appearance, or their relationship to the other characters in the book.

Further research for the parent-teacher

Conduct basic research (make summary notes) on:

- **The Harlem Renaissance** - an African-American art movement (1920 - 1930) that involved literature (Zora Neal Hurston), fine art, film (Oscar Micheaux) and photography (James Van Der Zee).

- **Autism and children with learning disabilities**

A Poetical Gift to You From the Tree

Our Communal Tree

We who are built of stone build again
Adorned by the meditative sun.

We who fly in astrological signs build again
Sculpting our orisha prayers for generations to read.

We who were once disfigured by a pirate's bible,
Make harp music to heal the souls of drowned hymns.

We who are built of white stone, build again
Adorned by the muse of a virgin winter.

We who made duel and took the gold, build again
Great castles of reparations? God will watch our truth.

We who built with Krishna's mad mantra, build again:
Not in ancient ruins but in the breath of invisible temples.

We who built with the dance of I Ching shells, build again,
Making calligraphy portraits to hang upon our communal Tree.

Stage 5- Learning Leadership Skills: the principles of success, the media and emotional literacy

Key words/themes: leadership, mindfulness and observing ones own thoughts

Aims
- To impress upon the parent-teacher the need for self-observation.
- To introduce the parent-teacher to the principles of success.
- To impress upon the parent-teacher the need to aquaint their child with mind games so as to develop life skills.
- To make the parent-teacher aware of the positive and negative influence of the media.

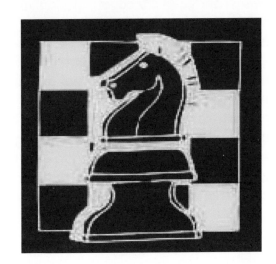

African Proverb

Man's greatest battles are the ones he
Fights within himself

Zambia

The art of teaching your child at Stage 5 is to act as if you have already achieved the goal; to observe your thoughts, especially when your habitual thoughts tell you that you can't achieve, or that your child can't achieve, or when you are visited by fear that stops you from taking positive action.

Often, you have to act as if you are the great Parent-Teacher. The education system sometimes baffles the average parent so much that they are at the mercy of an educational system that does not always see things from the point of view of the parent.

You have to play a key role in preparing your child for leadership. True leadership can only be enacted if you are free from bias, prejudice, discrimination. Thoughts based on past experiences that hold you back will limit your potential. Observe weak thoughts in yourself until they begin to fade away. When you find yourself in a tense situation, or loosing your temper, watch the thoughts in your mind, become aware of the tension spots in your body and remind yourself to breathe calmly. T

Breath, Courage and the Art of Self Observation

Your child's journey through the education system can prove stressful for both you and your child, so it is important that you stay relaxed, focused and in control of your emotional state.

Correct abdominal breathing, by increasing the oxygen to the brain, gives you mental clarity and courage, therefore we should spend some time looking at a simple breathing exercise. Each day find a quiet place to sit (preferably in the morning) and close your eyes, making sure you're totally relaxed and all tension is gone. The first step is to become aware that you are breathing and that your breathing needs to be rhythmic and slow. In observing your breathing notice the expansion and contraction of the rib cage, and as you do this visualise your lungs extending down from your rib cage right down to your stomach. With each inhalation imagine them being filled with air and positive energy, and when you breathe out imagine all your negative thoughts being exhaled. Once a regular breathing pattern is established simply start to concentrate on listening to the 'silence' of your breathing until this silence becomes real and peaceful. Practice this daily. Once you experience this silence regularly enough it will allow you to start living fully in the present, rather than thinking about the past or future, unless for practical requirements. With this new breathing pattern, with this silence emerging you will look at your child differently. You will observe yourself observing your child. This new awareness will allow you to discover their genius, and to create the silence and teach them this self-observation that they will need throughout their lives.

Mind Games

A mind game is a game that requires a great deal of thinking skills, including logic, guesswork and bluff. Mind games have been used since the ancient Egyptian times and their purpose was to develop mental skills and leadership. They were often combined with sports that had the same aim but where the focus was also on physical skills and strength.

A good mind game will combine the following:
a)   clear objective of what indicates a win
b)   mathematical calculations
c)   thinking skills
d)   strategies of offence
e)   strategies of defence
f)   mental discipline

At least one game must be learnt by the parent-teacher. If the parent- teacher does not know of any then they should learn with their child.
These mind games might be considered life skills. When playing these games tell your child how the mind games might mirror real life situations where they will need skills of negotiation, compromise and guile. Examples of mind games are chess, Oware and dominoes.
You might wonder why mind games should be part of this educational course. It is quite simple, childhood is being attacked from all sides, and if you are a parent unhappy with the choice of schools, the type of school, or your child faces a problem like bullying that isn't being addressed then you may have to battle through bureaucracy, tradition and prejudice. Here are some other issues that you might have to confront:

a)   Commercialism - advertisers are increasingly targeting the teen and pre-teen market, putting pressure on children and parents to purchase commercial goods.

b)   The internet - exposes the child to a variety of information (both good and bad) which can undermine both parenthood and childhood.

c)   The increased testing of children.

d)   Bullying - at Ebony we have had reported to us incidents of bullying in schools occurring more regularly, again resulting in stress for both parent and child.

So we can see that the parent-teacher and child will need an array of strategies to deal with a range of obstacles (challenges) in their journey to unlock the child's (and parent's) genius.

Ask yourself this: how have you prepared your child for 'failure', for the bully; for the stress of examinations, for the competitiveness of eventual work life? Your child has to learn the art of contemplation; the art of assertion and compromise; the difference between right and wrong. Your emotional awareness will teach him/her all of this.

How to Identify a Good Mind Game

The questions below will act as a checklist and help you establish good criteria for choosing a mind game for your child/family.

Criteria questions	Yes or No
Does the Mind Game involve mathematical calculations?	
Does the Mind Game involve a range of thinking skills?	
Is the Mind Game fun and entertaining?	
Is the Mind Game easy to learn?	
Does the Mind Game have an obvious eduational link/application? E.g., dominoes and mathematics	
Does the Mind Game teach strategies of offence, defence and compromise etc?	
Is this a family game i.e. can two or more players play it?	

Ten Principles of Success - Summary

Over the last seventeen years, I've interviewed hundreds of parents who have simply become stressed and frustrated in their fight to get their child into a better school, assessed, or some other issue which is undermining their child's education. In the book, *The Art of War for Executives* Donald G Krause outlines ten principles for success which the parent-teacher might wish to use as a strategy plan when fighting for a just cause to support their child's education.

- Learn to fight - because competition in life is inevitable. Fight for a good school for your child. Make your home school. Use this book to unlock your child's gen ius. Campaign for better educational facilities.
- Show the way - your leadership will determine success. Find a way to contribute to improving not only your child's educational opportunity, but that of others, and do this with humility.
- Do it right - right actions leads to success. So create the opportunity for success and take this action at the right time.
- Know the facts - get as much information as you possibly can in order to achieve success. Read, go on the internet; telephone your local education authority and get yourself as best informed as you possibly can.
- Expect the worse - if you have an educational issue that is not being addressed and you complain, do not expect your concerns to be addressed.
- Seize the day - take simple decisive action.
- Burn the bridges - don't look back and start having second thoughts.
- Pull together - liaise with others, get training and communicate with those who have similar interests and concerns regarding some aspect in education.
- Keep them guessing - when battling against injustice keep your strategy a mystery to those who you are battling against.

As a parent-teacher you must always have a strategy and this will make you realise that you are never defeated. Your child's education is the most important battle/ journey you will encounter. You might wish to see this whole book as part of your child's action plan, but an action plan is useless unless you adopt strategies to create a path for your child's education.

The Media: Empowerment or Disempowerment

Studies show that children who watch too much television and films, and violent media often experience the following negative affects:

1) They can often imitate the violence they witness in media.
2) Children seeing aggression being rewarded on television, might then use aggression as a strategy for getting what they want.
3) The high frequency of violence they see on television and films can desensitise them to the real consequence of violence.
4) Witnessing high levels of violence on television can affect the child's interpersonal skills, and even lead to anxiety and fears.

5) If the child experiences anxiety from the high levels of violence they see on television this in turn can affect their sleep pattern resulting in poor school performance.
6) Children under twelve years of age often can't distinguish between fantasy and reality, so violence witnessed on television in a fictional film might appear to them as real.

The most effective way to counter the bad influence of violence in media is by educating the parent and child on media literacy, so that they can critically assess all media within the home. It should be remembered however, that media can also play a very important role in educating the entire family, so it is a matter of monitoring and selecting positive media.

Research in America shows that black people watch television 72 hours per week, compared with the national average of 49 hours. In particular, black women watch television the most. For the black boy in a single led black female household, this means that his viewing habits are directed to satisfy feminine instincts.

The effects of watching television for the black child and young black viewer are:

a) Black children become programmed from an early age to become consumers and not producers of goods and services.
b) Television overpowers a child's sensitivity as they witness an average of 1800 acts of violence by the time they are 17 years of age.
c) White maleness is presented as the norm for the hero and acts of heroism.
d) A covert code of reference operates in media products to ensure black children underachieve and undervalue themselves.

Television Programmes that Show Underachievement and Ridicule

The typical western television schedule consists of the following television genres: the sitcom, the soap opera, current affairs, the quiz show, the chat/talk show, sports and reality shows. However, whilst we might think we are being entertained and informed we are often being miseducated. In the case of the sitcom class and race (mainly in British tv) is at the heart of the sitcom, so as a parent, if you truly want to prepare your child for a world where they can engage and celebrate the world's cultural diversity then you should analyse their viewing. Let's look at the sitcom and see exactly what we are laughing at.
The sitcom is usually defined as a sitcom genre by the following features:
• Comedy based genre
• Canned laughter
• Half an hour in duration
• Trivial story lines
• Each episode has a different story line which doesn't carry over to the next episode (normally)
• Set in a few central locations where all the actions take place
• Uses familiar stereotypes e.g. dumb blonde or silly foreigner
• Is episodic in structure

When we look at how the comedy is generated we find that more often than not it is generated by the 'intrusion' of an outsider, that is someone who is presented as not being part of the norm. In British comedy this has often been the foreigner, the black or social outcast. Secondly, comedy is sometimes generated by working class characters aspiring to be middle class.

In current affairs news programmes we see the portrayl of the so-called Third World as being dependents, riddled with corrupt government, suffering famine, ongoing civil wars and a place prone to natural disasters. There is never any explanation of how these situations arose. The Western media simply places the West as saviour: this Western world is led by white males.

In recent years we have seen the rise of Reality television programmes which are supposedly unscripted but are really scripted programmes, showing real life people in settings that create interpersonal conflicts and sexual tensions, which leads to supposedly spontaneous and authentic reactions from the non-celebrity participants of the shows. The audience is very carefully positioned as voyeurs, perhaps unaware that they are being manipulated by the programme makers.

So we can see that the blind consumption of television genres without any analysis can lead to the creation of a viewer that might not be entirely sure what they are laughing at, and one that is increasingly voyeuristic. The parent teacher should therefore be careful about what their child watches on tv, or at least explain to them the shortcomings of some television genres.

What You Should Do?

- Plan your child's television viewing.
- Set time limits of how much television your child can watch. The maximum television your child should watch should be no more than two hours per day.
- Make sure that your child does not watch excessive violence on television. Children can become desensitised to violence, not understanding that violence hurts, maims and kills.
- Make positive and informative comments as you watch television with your child.
- Educational television can have huge beneficial effects on pre-school children, so get educational videos, CDs etc.
- Children who are two years of age or below should not watch television other than educational television, as this can stop language development by preventing social interaction. Again, the parent should monitor the very young child's viewing.
- Studies show that children who watch too much television are likely to be over weight, do little exercise and indulge in frequent snacks of unhealthy food. When your child is watching television don't get them in the habit of eating junk food.

Tragedy of Childhood: Case Studies

It was March of '87. Somehow the winter had been thwarted early, and the sun had peeped out bringing its good news of optimism. Memory can be untrustworthy, but I remember this because I had come out bruised from a failed theatre production: artistically successful, but a financial disaster. This was how I got into education, not through any planned and virtuous ambition, but to get some financial stability behind me, and relief from the egos of theatre.

So it was in this month of colour that I arrived outside an unique, but oppressive educational centre, that was sprawled out over a corner of a south London housing estate. I had been taken on to be part of a multi-disciplinary team who worked with children who were not attending school regularly. Many of these children and young people had other issues like sexual or physical abuse, truancy and/or juvenile crime. The team that I was to be part of consisted of an educational psychiatrist, two other teachers and a social worker. It was like being cast in a 1960s play, for everyone seemed to be acting the role of therapist. This surrealism was further cemented when a colleague of mine, organised a young women's workshop to tackle their issues. To my amazement I saw her walk into the workshop brandishing a large bag of knitting and needle work. It confused me further. Yes, I thought to myself, I'm still in comedy theatre. But later I would learn that the young women enjoyed the project and had talked about other issues during the workshop. I later became convinced that those needles were pushed into the effigies of male management who had laughed at these workshops. The management team, who kept their distance from the young people, but wrote copious reports on these youngsters who they hardly knew, left the face to face work to the disgruntled youth workers. The person who was in charge of the centre was an ex-actress who strode around in her long dress, like a macabre character in an old black and white Hollywood film.

On my first day I was given piles of case files to read, which were so horrific; it made me scared to meet the young people in the centre, or should I say the young people that the files portrayed. The centre was a place where these children came on a temporary basis whilst their education and welfare were being assessed and sorted out; like getting them a new school, or new foster parent, or counselling regarding pregnancy. The centre acted as a bridge between schools and juvenile detention centres. Initially, I was impressed, especially when I attended the case meetings when everyone from social services, police, education came to take decisions as to the young person's future. But later, I would see that this centre with its oppressive fluorescent lighting was a place for deviance, and for those who studied deviance, yet had not studied it in themselves. Slowly, I began to question my role as the teacher. Was I simply providing basic education to give the system the veneer of caring when it was really a brutal system that incarcerated children because of their class or race? Was the basic skills I was supposed to be teaching them really basic skills?

The young people varied. Black, white, bright, not so bright, but nearly all had the father figure missing; and many seemed to be obsessed with some kind of sexual perversion. Often the boys would bring in pornographic material, and they'd boast about their sexual experiences. What they had in common was that they all wanted to escape from school. For a few of the children it seemed that it wasn't the usual additional issues (abuse, poverty, family break-up) that kept them from school. School didn't work, but the school authorities seemed reluctant to consider this. From the educational authority's point of view, these children were truants. No one could question the professional practice of the establishment. For a few of the young people I worked with I could see little hope of them successfully returning to school. Much of what I was being asked to do I simply didn't believe in. For me, it was the start of not simply looking for alternatives, but exploring other forms of more meaningful forms of education.

Those children are adults now. Chances are that they are all underachievers, that many would have had experiences of prison, poverty, drug addiction and unemployment. Now adults, some would have had children of their own, and it is more than likely that this new generation of children are having the same educational experiences as their parents. Who will break this cycle?

Moreover, who will heal these generations of children? Perhaps it's you, the parent-teacher, for the professional educator has to fall in line; has to defend established positions, has to protect salaries and jobs; has to teach in the context of short-sighted government educational policy; has to take new educational buzz words as if it were valium; has to be trained by people who themselves were mistrained: has to teach thirty children in a class, and has to stay in an industry that allows little time for research. The parent-teacher has a key role to play in the genuine revolution of education.

Further Research for the Parent-Teacher

Undertake basic research into:

a) Mind games of different cultures.
b) How children are influenced by media.

A Poetical Gift to You From the Tree

God-Shango, take this child,
And courage her sums,
To count the sticks of crippled legs,
And the additions of poverty's bones.

God-Shango, light this child of courage:
Let her reap your lullabye,
Before the war of adulthood,
And the unharvested food of world democracy.

God-Shango, teach her,
Why the plant isn't scared of vexed rain;
Why the tree isn't scared of thunder;
Why the great dance of Nature is her real victory.

Stage6 - Discipline and Learning: rites of passage models

Key words/themes: analysis, detachment, self-challenge and self awareness

Aims
- To introduce the parent-teacher to the importance of self-discipline.
- To make the parent-teacher aware of the link between motor-sensory activity and brain development.
- To introduce the parent-teacher to models for rites of passage programmes.

Self Awareness and Self Challenge

The art of teaching your child here is to analyse your child's learning without you becoming exasperated by their poor performance, or your child in some way not living up to your expectation. It is here that the self-challenge and self-awareness comes in because you have to watch your emotions all the time and therefore become *detached* from these emotions. This state of mind will allow you to remain focused and positive about your child's educational journey regardless of the barriers and obstacles that you come up against.

Movement and Learning

The neural network in the body has to be stimulated by movement. The modern child spends an increasing number of hours per week being driven from home to school, and sitting at home watching tv, videos, or playing a computer game. As a result, this neural network is not being stimulated and therefore the brain becomes slow in its operations.

What you must do:

➢ You must have your child do some aerobic activity like sports, dance etc. (Remember the brain needs oxygen)
➢ You must engage your child in a sports activity at least twice per week.

Activity

Here is a self-challenge table that should be used weekly.

Challenge and tasks	Yes or No
6-8 glasses of water (daily)	
Wholesome diet	
Education research	
Quality time with family	
Monitored my children's watching of the television (plus PC games)	
Completed lesson from *How To Unlock My Child's Genius*	
Spoken to my child about their school work or/and liaised with the school	

Rites of Passage Models and The Circle of Courage

The term rites of passage was first termed by Arnold Van Gennep, the French anthropologist in the early part of the 20th century. This term has come to mean the journey that a young person takes through various stages in their life. The preparation for this journey is usually sanctioned by the community, who want their young people to be prepared for adulthood and additional responsibilities. The Jewish bar mitzvahs fulfil many functions of the rites of a passage programme. As there is now growing concern about what is happening to today's children and young people in terms of gangs, underachievement, bullying, child abuse, drug addiction, truancy, teen pregnancy and even suicide, more and more groups are calling for programmes that will help young people prepare for adulthood. In this section I will simply put forward a basic model of how you might shape your rites of passage programme.

The Design

It is important when designing a rites of passage programme that you:

- Undertake research. Look at other models and perhaps adapt them to your needs.
- Consult with the young people who the programme is aimed at.
- Consult with the wider community and parents who the children/young people belong to.
- The programme might involve the child/young person being temporarily isolated from their parents but you should of course ensure safety, trained personnel and the necessary police checks.
- Make the assignments task orientated.
- Train both mentor and mentee.

The Aims of a Rites of Passage Programme

- To prepare the child/young person for different and challenging stages in their life.
- To prepare the child/young person for new responsibilities.
- To allow the community to acknowledge the child's/young person's transitional stage and achievement.
- To give the child/young person survival skills.
- To give the child/young person knowledge of their community's values, customs and aspirations.
- To allow the child/young person the opportunity to master a skill.

What does the mentee get from a rites of passage programme?

- Allows them to feel that they are part of a group.
- Raises their self-esteem and confidence.
- Allows them the opportunity to be further respected for their achievement.
- At the adolescent stage it allows the young person to fulfil their instinctive desire to face a challenge, prove their physical prowess, become a hero and be accepted by the wider community.

Duration of a Rites of Passage Programme

The duration of these rites of passage programmes can vary, but there should be build-up and follow-up workshops to support the child/young person. The duration can be from one day to a year depending on the focus and resources of the programme.

As this book is largely an educational programme you might wish to design your programme around both educational and social targets and achievements, such as changing school, passing an exam, learning a new skill, starting a new school as well as the transition from boyhood/girlhood to manhood/womanhood.

The Mentor in the Rites of Passage Programme

Some groups advertise for mentors and whilst the success of this approach varies, the above model can be used within a small family or community group where the mentor can be a relative, family friend, uncle etc. This has the added advantage of giving that person a role and responsibility in their community. In addition to this it demonstrates to the mentor that they can contribute, and it might well tap into their latent talents. Training should be given to the mentor, and this book could be the guide for a training course.

The role of the mentor is to:
- Act as a confidant to the child/young person.
- Help deliver the rites of passage programme.
- Act and give guidance.
- Share their experience of life skills.
- Be a role model for the child/young person.
- Represent the values and expectations of the wider community.
- Have good communications skills and be able to gain the child's/young person's trust.

An example of what might be expected in one of these programmes

- Peer pressure (bullying) and lifestyle
- Media and youth culture
- Drugs awareness
- Cultural history
- Family, community and identity
- Sexual awareness

The last point is that rites of passage programmes must be backed-up with good administration, inventiveness and commitment. If the child/young person's community does not provide them with these types of programmes then the under-resourced and misguided street gang will.

Further research for the parent-teacher

Conduct basic research into:

- The social and cultural significance of the mind game Oware.
- The educational use of mind games in non-Western countries.
- How various models of rites of passage programmes are used in different parts of the world.

A Poetical Gift to You From the Tree

Young Warrior

Young warrior,
Truth will be your torment and saviour,
As you battle armed with an old candle

See the battlefield,
Arched over you like old Solomon,
Wicked and wretched

Young warrior,
Where are the keys,
To doors of genius and wonder.

Step 7: Holistic Education: complimentary therapy and financial literacy

Key words/phrases: holistic; give and seek nothing in return; interrelationships

Aims
- To make the parent-teacher aware of the holistic approach to education.
- To introduce the parent-teacher to the idea of the learning zone.
- To introduce the parent-teacher to the educational uses of complimentary therapy.
- To make the parent-teacher aware of the issues around financial literacy.

African Proverb
It takes a whole village to raise a child

The art of teaching your child at this stage is about developing their whole brain. Various models are used which portray the brain as left hemisphere and right hemisphere, triune brain etc. What these models attempt to do is demonstrate that different parts of the brain are responsible for different functions, and that the development of the brain has resulted in higher and lower thinking/understanding. At this stage you must stimulate your child's learning with assignments that require them to use the whole brain. The learning assignments here should include:
- Pictures
- Colour
- Shape and imagery
- Holistic thinking skills
- Imaginative/creative
- Rhythm
- Humour

The work you did in Stage 4 of this book began to teach you the art of observation. In step 7 we are looking at observing interrelationships and interdependencies. By studying nature you will observe hidden intelligences. This fosters and encourages the mind of inquiry.
Features of the mind of inquiry:
a)   the mind is quiet
b)   understanding beyond thought

c)   understanding of cycles
d)   understanding of patterns in nature
e)   the contemplative mind
f)   understanding of natural harmony

Let's imagine that one day you get up and look out of your window over your garden (or your local park) and you see the heavy rain falling whilst great roars of thunder and lightening crack the sky. A few moments later there is peace. A magical rainbow appears, the grass glistens with this fresh rain; the sun peeps out; snails have been coerced from crevices, and the air is full of lush smells of greenery. Imagine this. Observe this right now in your imagination. What pockets of science are you able to discern? What are the interconnections between these phenomena? I am not trying to make you into a Nobel scientist, simply to make you aware of nature, and your awareness, your fascination and your enquiry will influence your child. It will lead you to seek out ecological projects in your local community and wider your child's understanding of the natural world.

As Stage 7 involves teaching the whole child, such an ambitious task can only be achieved by the community. It is arrogant to think that one individual or one institution can achieve this. In order to give your child experiences, opportunities and the variety and freedom to learn you have to create a Learning Zone. What is a learning zone? Well you probably already have one in some kind of embryonic form, but you need to realise its potential, utilise its resources and imaginatively engage in it.

A learning zone is a network of local resources accessible to you and your child, that can aid both formal and informal learning. In particular, this learning zone has the opportunity to use education and culture as a teaching strategy. The voluntary sector has tremendous resources that can be tapped into.

a)   the local museum
b)   a relative or trusted friend who is good at storytelling
c)   a relative or trusted friend who can teach a cultural craft like steel pan making, quilt making, puppet theatre etc
d)   local Saturday School
e)   local cultural festivals
f)   Black History Month celebrations
g)   a children's yoga club
h)   Kwanzaa celebrations
i)   International Women's Day celebrations
j)   Chinese New Year Festival

Create a Learning Zone diary to plan and attend these identified events. Other community teachers lie dormant in communities, unaware of their role, responsibility or genius. Make sure that you tell them about this educational programme that you and your child have engaged in.

Complimentary Therapy and Education

Bach Flower Remedies

Dr. Edward Bach (1886 - 1936) 'discovered' the healing energies of selected flow-ering plants and trees. He wanted to treat his patients with non toxic and gentle substances which took into account the persons emotional state. Dr. Bach believed that disease was the result of conflict between our spiritual and mortal sides. These 38 remedies he 'discovered 'are divided into seven groups, with each group representing conflicts within us and which stop us fulfilling our potential. The seven Bach flower groups are:

• Fear
• Uncertainty
• Disinterest in present circumstances
• Loneliness
• Over-sensitivity
• Despondency or despair
• Worry about other people's welfare

Below are some remedies that are useful in addressing emotional problems that a child might have. The table below is obviously not a diagnosis of any kind. The reader should contact a qualified and registered practitioner if they wish to have a diagnosis.

Emotional State	Treatment
Puberty	Walnut
Being a victim	Centary
Being a bully	Vine & Sunflower
Being over-active	Vervain & Bluebell
Shy and timid	Mimulus & Borage
Cannot learn	Chestnut Bud, Tansy
Children who lack confidence	Larch or Buttercup
Children who are sulky	Willow
Children who are jealous of younger siblings	Holly
Children who need constant attention	Chicory
First aid treatment (shock, tension, trauma, terror)	Rescue remedy

Remedies to Support the Parent-Teacher

Emotional State	Remedy/ies
The parent who cannot cope	Elm
The over anxious parent	Red Chestnut
The stressed parent	Cherry Plum &/or Vervain
The exhausted parent	Olive &/or oak

The impatient parent	Impatiens
The over-critical parent	Beech
The possessive parent	Chicory
First aid (trauma, tension, terror)	Rescue Remedy

Homoeopathy and Education

Modern homoeopathy was started by Samuel Hahneman (1755 - 1843). Hahneman first used the word homoeopathy in 1807 which was derived from two Greek words, homoios meaning similar and pathos meaning suffering. The name is therefore in accordance with the homoeopathic principle of treating like with like. Homoeopathy uses medicines derived from plant, mineral and animal sources. Healing systems like homoeopathy seek to stimulate the body's own resources to heal itself. We can therefore say that homoeopathy seeks to understand and deal with the underlying health issues of the patient. Homoeopathy is a holistic therapy which recognises each patient to be unique, therefore the practitioner studies the patient's mental, physical and emotional condition.

In order to benefit from homoeopathy you must go to a qualified and registered practitioner. Below are some guidelines that can help you to be more informed when you visit the homoepath to get your child's remedy.

The visit to the homoeopath will take about one hour. The homoeopath will seek to establish a profile of the patient by asking questions and taking notes around:
- Patient history
- Physical characteristics
- Mental Characteristics
- Emotional characteristics
- Sensitivity to weather

From this profile the homoeopath will seek to match a constitutional remedy to the profile of the child.

Dr D. M. Borland made a study of remedies suitable for children and identified five groups, which I now present as an introduction to the usefulness of homoeopathic remedies for children.

Group	Child Profile	Remedy
Group 1	Lack of energy; lethargic; slow closure of fontanelles; sluggish mentally and physically; slow at school and games; wants to sit and do nothing; sensitive to criticism.	Calcarea Carbonica **Other remedies in this group:** Calcarea Phos; Phosphorus; Silica; Lycopodium; Causticum.
Group 2	For children who are late in speaking, walking, gaining weight	Baryta Carbonica Other remedies in this group:

		and who are small for their age. Tend to be shy, nervous, forgetful and lack concentration	Borax; Nat Mur; Sepia; Aurum; Carbo Vegetabalis.
Group 3		Fat, heavy child with large head; muscular weakness, rheumatoid pains; timid; lack assurance; harsh dry skin; acute acne in antimonium; adolescents; sleepy during the day; constipation.	Graphites Other remedies from this group: capsicum; psorinum; petroleum; crudum.
Group 4		Two types of Pulsatilla children. First one is shy, slight, sensitive; loving. The second type is fatter, sluggish, weepy; craves attention. Both have digestive problems; chilly during fever; sleeps with hands over head	Pulsatilla **Other remedies in the group:** sulphur; thuja; iodine; floric acid.
Group 5		Nervy, delicate, frightened of the dark; night terrors; highly distressed; digestive upsets due to the cold; headaches at school.	Arsenicum Other remedies in this group: chamomillia; cina; magnesia carbonica; ignatia; zincum.

Financial Literacy

Children having credit cards is now common in many countries, and therefore there is growing concern about children building up debt on these cards. Parents and educators are now calling for financial literacy to be considered as a basic skill. In America children between 8 - 14 years control a budget of $39 billion, and billions more through their influence on parents. As a result of this, marketing companies are now targeting children, knowing that they will in turn put pressure on their parents to purchase certain goods and services.

The parent-teacher must play an active role in developing good financial skills and awareness in their children. So lets start by looking at three basic financial concepts about money which we can start with to begin to develop good financial literacy.

▪ Spending
What will you spend your money on? Who will you spend it with? Why will you spend your money? What are your spending patterns? Have you given your child a budget regarding the uses of their spending, and discussed the implications of getting into debt?

- Saving

Has your child a saving plan? Are the principles of saving being taught to your child? Does your saving plans have clear aims?

- Sharing

Will you share your money with others who are less fortunate? Will you teach your child moral values around sharing and how to use money in their lives?

Joline Godfrey, in her book *The Ten Basic Money Skills*, identifies ten lessons that children/young people need, to know on good money management, which are:

1. How to save.
2. How to keep track of money.
3. How to get paid what you are worth.
4. How to spend your money wisely.
5. How to talk about money.
6. How to live on a budget.
7. How to invest.
8. How to exercise the entreprenurial spirit.
9. How to handle credit.
10. How to use money to change the world.

Godfrey goes on to divide the stages of a person's life into five stages: Apprenticeship stage (5 - 18); starting out stage (19 - 30); taking charge stage (31 - 50), and the Third Wave (66 onwards). Interestingly, Godfrey says that financial literacy is about economic self-defense, and this is precisely how my parent's generation viewed it back in the late 1940s and 1950s.

In 1948 the *SS Empire Windrush* sailed from the Caribbean to England carrying 498 West Indians who had been encouraged to come to Britain to help re-build the country after the second world war. On arrival many of the young immigrants, having worked hard and having young families, wanted to purchase a home but many of the building societies would not give them a loan simply because they were black immigrants. They were forced to come together and pool their resources. They started operating *esu su hand*, an economic saving schemes that actually originated from Africa; a system (or Partner as called in Jamaica) which saw small groups of ten to thirty people contribute a small sum of money each week, with one of them taking all the money when it was their turn. They bought big old houses that the indigenous white community did not want, and then they would rent out a few rooms in the house as a source of income. This was their source of economic self-defence, but it would be later undermined as the following generation did not maintain these schemes and sought to use the financial services of other communities.

Financial literacy is important not only for the child in knowing how to handle their credit card, but in understanding how wealth is created in the world, how wealth is secured, maintained and why there is world debt. Crisis upon crisis will force them to ask why a third of the world's natural wealth has been wasted away due to over-consumption; where does the Western nations of the world get their resources to pursue such a rich lifestyle and the fairness of this system. They must be made aware of their responsibility as future world citizens in ending debt and poverty.

Further Research for the Parent-Teacher

Undertake basic research into the following:
- Homoeopathy and childhood illnesses
- Bach flower remedies for children
- Financial literacy for children

A Poetical Gift From the Learning Tree to You

Lady Maat

Look pon Lady Maat
Wid she big hat
People say she 'ave no money
And she foot stay funny
And she always carrying scales
Take care police don't carry her to jail.

Hear big people shout!

Don't knock her door,
She ugly and she poor

Children reply:

But us children don't care
How can old woman make us fear

Lady Maat:

I am Lady Maat
De old woman wid feather in she hat;
Who god give trick and magic
To fling pon de weak and sick.

Now big big people vex:

Go' bout your business you silly old crow
You black and mad, your back bend-up like a bow.

The poor children sing:

We are de children of de street:
No family, no clothes, or shoe pon we feet.
We ask no favours or trust

Just likkle food, or a piece of crust.

And Lady Maat
Took off her big hat
Welcomed them in
Wid one warm sweet grin

I bless you each wid a smile,
And you must bless others too.
So like Lady Maat wid she big hat
Gave dem love and didn't seek anyt'ing back

Step 8: Education and Culture: adapting kwanzaa

Key words and themes: structure, planning, cycles; culture and education

Aims
- To develop strategies of educational planning.
- To establish education targets for your child.
- Reinforce the power of positive affirmations.

When most parents see this education course they tend to say I don't have the time to do all this work to support my child. I work full time! But the truth is they do have the time but they simply do not have the time management skills to implement this programme. In order to address this the parent-teacher has to make a daily *Things to Do List* coupled with a list of their goals. Below is a model.

Task	Priority	Activity	By When	Completed
Goals				
Goal 1				
Goal 2				
Goal 3				

Positive Affirmation
I am the great Parent-Teacher. I am unlocking my child's genius

The above strategy of Things to Do List, continuously writing down your goals and the positive affirmation will help you to plan this programme. It will not only make you achieve more but also improve your quality of life because you will have more time for your child, yourself and your community.

The art of teaching your child at this stage is to make them understand structure and planning. What you have been doing in this programme is creating an education plan, but what you have to understand and do is take this education plan and make it fit their life plan.

➢ Encourage your child observe the structure and plan of nature. Simple science projects are very good for this.
➢ Encourage your child to make a weekly things to do plan if they are old enough.
➢ Encourage them to write down exactly where they want to be in life and encourage ambition.

The *Summary Year Planner* below will help you to plan your child's year and anticipate events that could cause problems, but also allows you to support your child during times of change.

Summary Year Planner

	Semester/Term 1	Semester/Term	Semester/Term 3
Academic	• First Day • Parents Evening • School trip • New friends made	• Mid-year tests • Possible change of friends	• End of year tests • End of year report • School play
Cultural/ Religious	• Christmas	• Kwanzaa • Chinese New year	
Personal (Complete these sections)			

Education and Culture

As our theme and mission is education and unlocking the genius of the child, it is important that we take every opportunity to support our children's education by incorporating culture into the event. At Ebony we have used the Kwanzaa celebrations as a celebration of learning. This strategy can be used in any cultural event. The advantages of this approach are:
▪ The community acknowledge the achievements of the child/children.
▪ Being a non-academic experience there is a sense of celebration.
▪ The community openly supports the achievement of the child/children.

- The event acts as a rites of passage gathering, as it acknowledges the transition in terms of life skills of the child/children.
- The event educates the child/children as to their responsibility in building up their community.
- It reminds the child/children that the community has invested in their education and therefore their education is not about personal achievement but community achievement.

Kwanzaa Celebrations and Education

Kwanzaa is an international black cultural holiday that celebrates, community, family values and cultural heritage. The festival was started by Dr. Maulana Karenga, who based the holiday on ancient African harvest celebrations. Kwanzaa (which means first fruits) is celebrated over seven days, that is, from 26th December to 1st January. In African culture this is called 'when the edges of the year meet'.

Kwanzaa celebrates seven principles:
1. Umoja - (Unity) which means to work for unity and maintain this unity in the community, family, nation and race. This takes place on 26th December.
2. Kujichaguilia - (Self-determination) this means to define ourselves, name ourselves, and speak to ourselves. This takes place on 27th December.
3. Ujima - (Collective work and responsibility) this means to collectively build and maintain our community. This takes place on 28th December.
4. Ujamaa - (Co-operative Economics) to build and maintain our own businesses and to profit collectively. This takes place on 29th December.
5. Nia - (Purpose) To dedicate ourselves to the purpose of restoring our people to their former greatness. This takes place on 30th December.
6. Kuumba - (Creativity) - to create beautiful and beneficial cultural legacies.
7. Imani (Faith) to believe in our parent-teachers, teachers and leaders, and in our struggle and victory. This takes place on 1st January.

The Seven Symbols of Kwanzaa

1. Karamu crops
2. Mkeka (m-kay-cah) - mat
1. Kinara (kee-nah-rah) - candle holder
2. Mishumaa Saba (mee-shoo-maa) - seven candles
3. Muhinidi (moo-hee-dee) - ears of corn
4. Zawadi (Sah-wah-dee) - gifts
5. Kikoombe Cha Umoja (Kee-coam-bay chah-oomoe-jah) - unity cup

At Ebony we have held Kwanzaa on a single day due to the school calendar, so you can do this if it is more convenient or you can have the event over the official seven days. I also created the Kwanzaa Queen as the personification of Kwanzaa's principles so that the children could identify with the celebrations. She explains the overall event, gives out the gifts, leaves cultural legacies and generally permeates the festival so as to stir the children's imagination.

Each day might start with a welcoming, a short statement of intention, purification and libation.

Below are some suggestions how you might adapt an established cultural event and make it into an education and empowerment festival. *Remember, the Learning Tree is the central symbol.*

Day 1 - Theme - Unity

Organise a family trip to a cultural event that promotes family learning. Family learning is about the whole family learning about a subject, where each member has a role and learns at their own pace when the final outcome is a shared learning experience. Take the family to a play, exhibition or local community event. If applicable and possible, undertake research. Prepare some worksheets to be completed on the event. Prepare special food; take photos and record the event. For too many years I have interviewed families wanting to send their child/ren to one of my schools, and seen a dispirited and isolated single parent, not knowing which way to turn to get support for their child's education. So create some unity in the family; gather friends, cousins and engage in some *edutainment.*

Day 2 - Kujichagulia (Self-Determination)

Identify a great figure who strove to determine the course of history for their group. Examples might be Nelson Mandela (South Africa) or Mother Thereasa. Study their life. Try and get pictures, books, music and even CDs on them. Another key feature in identifying your person of 'self-determination' is that they should have started in humble means and little education opportunities. This will serve to inspire all who celebrate this aspect of Kwanzaa. Someone who I celebrate each year is Dr. John Henrik Clarke, the African-American historian. There is a very good film on his life entitled, *'A Great and Mighty Walk'.*

Day 3 Ujima - Collective Work and Responsibility

In most communities one of the biggest problems is education. Gatherings, should discuss ways to address this issue of education, resulting in an agreed and pre-planned action plan.

Day 4 Ujamaa - Co-operative Economics

Your education plan will need a financial plan. The gathering of people who have come together should make a donation as a gesture of support. Investigate community financial schemes like Sous Sous Hands, investment clubs, church/religious funds. Invite those who have started community businesses to announce and present their success. You could even celebrate a business plan to start a school.

Day 5 Nia - Purpose

The purpose of the celebrations is to build a better tomorrow. Uplifting and visionary poetry, songs and art etc can be used. This art should come from all generations on an agreed theme - purpose.

Day 6 Kuumba - Creativity

On this day cultural legacies should be exhibited. People of genius express this in their art, regardless of the appalling poverty they might find themselves in. But the art must be empowering, a response to the needs of the people, be it political, social or spiritual. Indeed the Learning Tree demands all of this and more.

An exhibition might be staged by community artists, but it is important that workshops with children take place so that the art is not removed from them and their families understanding.

Acknowledge the hard work the children have completed over the year and give them gifts not only for their academic work but also for their personal development.

Day 7 Imani - Faith
Courage and vision is needed at this stage. Now that your Tree has flourished, seeds must be planted for the year to come. Show gratitude for the fruits that the Tree has made you taste or perceive, and give thanks to that which is greater than you for life.

End your celebrations with a final statement, or prayer, or affirmation as you gather around your Learning Tree.

Further Research for the Parent-Teacher

Undertake basic research into:
• Personal time management

A poetical gift to you the Parent-teacher from the Tree

Toast For Dem Old People
(For the old West Indians and other immigrants who made the journey to England in the 1950s and planted the ancestral Trees)

Let we toast dem old people;
Remember dem broom working de street,
Cursing it find and interruption.

Let we raise we glass,
Though shame drop we head;
And let strong rum give we strength.

Let we toast we sweet people dem,
Who we bring flower and respect for:
Who did out there in winter snow,
Sweeping up frozen tear and ambition.
Old people, you reach heaven yet?
Dem does lick domino like we?
Man, time your hard work retire:
We hear heaven clean and tidy,
Like veranda back home.
Let we toast we old friends,
'Cause God will tolerate dem head.
Poor t'ing, dem old people dead.

Stage 9- Thinking Skills and Barriers to Learning: race, class and learning difficulties and abilities

Key words & phrases: wisdom; to resolve conflicts; to be quiet and still your thoughts

Aims
- To introduce to the parent basic strategies of resolving conflict.
- To introduce the parent-teacher to issues around race, class, learning difficulties and abilities.
- To introduce the parent-teacher to the role of thinking skills in their child's development.

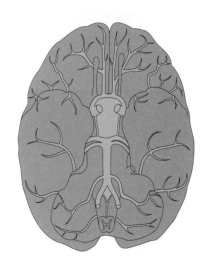

African Proverb
The wise create proverbs for fools to learn, not to repeat
        Ghana

The art of teaching here to is resolve all your conflicts so that you are not imposing your conflicts, your anxieties on your child. The resolution of conflict can only be achieved by the mind becoming quiet; by you watching the noise and chatter that keeps talking in your mind. This will lead to a greater peaceful state of mind and allow you to become more aware of issues in your child's life.

Some suggestions:
➤ Avoid ongoing arguments
➤ Try not to be quarrelsome, otherwise you will teach your child to act this way
➤ Resolve all family arguments by the end of the day
➤ Try and make the house quiet
➤ Teach your child to respect and appreciate silence

Tension

Tension is the result of:
a)   improper breathing
b)   poor posture
c)   negative thoughts
d)   poor diet
e)   hectic lifestyle

The above will result in the parent-teacher experiencing a poor emotional and physical state which means that in dealing with issues on your child's education you under-perform through incorrect thinking. To correct this you have to:

a)   make sure you breathe from your abdomen and not in the upper chest.

b)   become more aware of your posture e.g., stop yourself slouching.

c)   use simple positive affirmations to make yourself joyful.

d)   visualise yourself constructively in a lifestyle change that sees you upgrading your skills to become a parent-teacher.

e)   make sure that you have a healthy diet. Research into organic foods, vegan foods; increase your intake of raw foods and shop more creatively.

f)   Engage in time management to enable you to isolate quality time for you to practice activities that allow for quiet contemplation, health rejuvenation and enjoyment.

By following the above you are able to contemplate on the particular education (or other) issue. By simply breathing and visualising the positive outcome.

From contemplation to meditation

Meditation is a state between (or in the middle) the waking state and the sleeping state. The meditation state in induced by an increase in oxygen and the slowing down of the rate of breathing. The slower the breath, the slower the thoughts in your awareness. The perseverance of this state leads to detachment, insight and relaxation.

Meditation involves:

- Deep breathing (rhythmic)
- Quiet observation of thoughts
- Awareness of breath
- Positive visualisation
- Mindfulness
- Chanting in some cases

Once this state of peacefulness is experienced regularly then the parent-teacher is able to handle issues around their child's education with a great deal more insight, tact and less emotionalism. This contemplative mind stops the parent-teacher becoming stressed. Conflicts between child and parent-teacher are more easily resolved, and the child does not imitate negative behaviour copied from the parent.

Thinking Skills

In *'How to Teach Your Child How To Think'* Edward de Bono states that almost all the thinking taught in schools is reactive thinking which fits in the Western tradition. Reactive means that something is put in front of the student and they simply have to react to it. There are no new thinking models or designs used. He goes on to point out that real life thinking involves a great deal of proactive thinking which means going out and doing things. But we might add to Mr de Bono's comments and say that great 'thinking' is about observing the thinking process itself, which leads to true learning about the self, and is the art of disciplined learning.

He calls for thinking skills that are constructive, creative and generative. In the western society this reactive thinking has simply resulted in an adversarial system; that is, an argument is simply 'explored' through argument, debate and protest. Research into other non-Western cultures (Sternberg and Grigorenko), show that intelligence skills are based around:

1) academic intelligence
2) social qualities (respect, responsibility and consideration)
3) practical thinking
4) comprehension

We can see that the thinking that your child learns/imitates in school is limited and insufficient to assist in them unlocking their genius. If we want to look at good thinking skills we might start at looking at what prevents good thinking. To improve your thinking skills you should:

- Think without the involvement of the ego.
- Engage in practical thinking
- Use thinking tools.
- Observe your own thinking

Thinking Exercises for the Teacher-Parent and the Child

You can use the Learning Tree and make it real by looking at the tree (and thinking) in your garden, or local park or even simply drawing one. It is important that you do one of these exercises as the Learning Tree will become the focus of these thinking skills both directly and indirectly. Talk about this learning Tree, make it colourful; explore its magical world, its seasons; the Tree as a habitat for small creatures; the Tree as a place for both you and your child to seek solace, quiet contemplation and inspiration. It is an old Ghanaian tradition that when you go under a tree you should ask the tree's permission to use its space. You are simply allocating quality thinking and contemplation, to a traditional natural place.

Your child should see you go to the Learning Tree when you want to work out an issue. They see your body language, they see you challenged but you don't get angry. You go to your genius and the answer comes. Under your Tree you breathe, you observe your thoughts and you decide which thinking skill to use.

Develop Your Own Thinking Tools

The simplest way to start doing this is to change your language, which in turn changes your opinions and beliefs. You can for example refer to yourself in the third person, i.e., instead of calling yourself me, or I, you can simply say the parent-teacher. This leads to a detachment.
- Use doodle-thinking designs to tackle practical problems: pictures, or diagrams can be used. A small book should be carried around. See each thinking activity as a challenge.

- For difficult thinking problems do not persist if an immediate solution does not come. Try and draw the problem, and literally sleep on it. The answer will come from the brain's ability to naturally resolve issues.

Once you start working on your thinking skills encourage your child's thinking skills. You will have already started them on mind games but now set them tasks in the home and community. For example, depending on your child's age delegate duties to them that require them to organise visits to the theatre or music show, or let them prepare (supervised) a meal.

Barriers to Your Child's Genius

- Race
- Class
- Learning Difficulties and Disabilities

Race as a barrier

The main barrier to the black and ethnic minority child fulfilling their true potential is racism.

What is racism?

When one racial group has power (economic, social etc) and discriminates against another group to maintain and increase this power, and uses race as a way to oppress another group, then a system of racism has been established. In order to continue to maintain this power the racist group creates a whole cultural mythology about its superiority and denigrates the group it suppresses and continues to exploit that group. This mythology further disempowers the oppressed group. Racism affects all aspects of society and is present in institutions like education, health and business.

What is the Thinking Design Behind Racism and How Does it Impact in Your Child's Education?

Racism operates from a self-centred thinking pattern, which means that the world is seen in a segregative way; therefore, there is constant division, opposition and conflict. The education system continues to point the blame of underachievement at the victims. At parent-evenings the teachers articulate this with comments such as:

- *..must try harder..*
- * has fallen behind..*
- *..doesn't quite grasp concepts..*
- *..needs to concentrate more..*
- *..lacks confidence..*
- *..he/she's having problems*
- *..tries hard but doesn't quite understand..*
- *..good at sports though..*

94

The victim is blamed for their underachievement! This is another feature of the thinking pattern of racism.

We end up with various categories of underachievers:
- the excluded child
- the excluded adult who ends up in prison
- the truant
- the child that is bullied
- the child with a supposed learning disability
- the shy child

The underachieving child might well become the underachieving adult who may even end up in prison. There is a link between illiteracy, truancy, learning disability and crime.

In the book *The Black and White Media Show*, (Ed. J Twitchin) it is outlined how a school can be institutionally racist and damage both black and white children by:
1. Marginalising the interests of black and ethnic minority communities.
2. Making tokenist gestures towards black and ethnic minority communities.
3. Assuming black and ethnic minority conform to stereotypes.
4. Refusal to change or reform in the interests of all the communities.
5. Being patronising to black and ethnic minority families.
6. Adopting an assimilationist approach by treating black and ethnic minority children as if they are white.
7. By denying black and ethnic minority communities access to the power structure of the school.
8. Doing little to build success, or challenge, or evaluate practices that are not working.

A school may actually be implementing many positive policies to alleviate racism but still, the black and ethnic minority child does not succeed because the teacher is not ambitious for the child. Underachievement is therefore programmed into the psychology of the child and any remedial action, therefore becomes so difficult to prescribe due to the covert nature of this type of racism.

The black and ethnic minority communities in desperation shout for more black and ethnic minority teachers. But the black and ethnic minority teacher is underachieving as much as the students. Small attempts are made to address the situation, but with each step progress is hindered by the attitude of those who believe:
- *We shouldn't celebrate Black History Month, it's racist!*
- *They only got the job (the black or ethnic minority teacher) because they're black!*
- *It's street culture that's holding them back.*

The Euro-centric education system teaches that the western intellectual tradition started with the Greeks, when in fact many Greeks themselves (Herodotus, Strabo and Plutarch) say that they learnt their knowledge from the Egyptians. History as taught in schools does not teach that the Greeks actually went to study in Egypt (Thales, Pythagoras and Democritus were all taught by those who were taught by

Egyptian priests, and that the Egyptians were black Africans). This in turn would mean that the study of African Egyptian mathematics, logic, astronomy, engineering, architecture and philosophy would have to be placed in a black cultural/spiritual context. In addition, the black child studying this material would appreciate the genius of their ancestors, and would respect and seek that same knowledge.

The Way Forward?

How can the black and ethnic minority child succeed? By building an education system where the thinking design is not based on the segregative pattern of the racist model. The parent-teacher, and their community, must use an inclusive thinking design to build a holistic education system.

Class as a barrier

Class is still a major barrier to children achieving their full potential. Only 14 per cent of young people from working class backgrounds go to university in Britain, compared with 75 per cent from middle class and wealthy homes. According to a report in The Observer (November 10, 2002) *Britain's Class Divide*, starts even before nursery school. This destructive class system is set at nursery stage. Other reports put the figure of working class going to university at only 7 per cent. Again, like racism, it will have to be working class communities themselves who will have to initiate education and child/young people programmes (as outlined in this book) that will address this issue.

Learning Difficulties and Disabilities

Children with learning difficulties and disabilities covers:
* Children who are deaf or partially hearing
* Children who are blind or partially sighted
* Children who have mental health problems
* Children who are dyslexic and related specific learning difficulties
* Children with physical disabilities
* Children with learning difficulties
* Children with autistic spectrum disorders

Very often the barrier to these children achieving is ignorance from the wider community and even the education institution which these children attend. Good practice is a key to helping these children achieve and this includes:
* Treat the child as an individual and not a condition
* Don't assume you know what the full implications of the disability are.
* Understand the social dimension of the disability.
* Be aware of attitudes to your child, e.g., patronising behaviour.
* Develop a positive learning environment in the home (hopefully using the Genius programme).
* Reflect on what strategies or resources you have used which works for your child.

- If your child has difficulty with concentration, plan short learning exercises and allow them to take breaks.
- Ensure that you know your child's entitlement for assessments or exams e.g., extra time for examinations.
- Know your child's learning style.

Using Technology

Children with learning difficulties often benefit from computers, and it can benefit visually impaired children. Using a computer can take away the fear that a child might have of making mistakes. Specialist software can increase the learning opportunities and improve the child's computer skills.

Further Research for the Parent-Teacher

Undertake basic research into:

- Thinking skills that you and your child can use.
- Racism, or class, or the relevant learning difficulty/disability, in education.

A Poetical Gift to You From the Tree

Keep Your Smile My Child

Keep your smile my child;
Even when they denounce your genius,
For they don't see your sleep;
Hear the truth of your prayers.
Did you not save the world in your play?

Keep your smile my child,
When tears torment;
When those dragons of peace
Point you to illiteracy.
Scribble your genius and graffiti the universe.

Keep your smile my child.
Your veiled blessings are all the world has.

Stage 10 - Community Education: e-learning and family learning

Key words: The Great You and the Great Curriculum

Aims:
- To introduce the parent-teacher to family learning, e-learning and the feminine principle of education.

African Proverb
No matter how big a child is, he
cannot deny that he was once carried
On the back of a woman
Nigeria

The art of teaching your child at stage 10 is to discover your own greatness and that of your child. Your observations will lead you to the insight that you are the great teacher of life skills, because you have observed yourself and therefore allowed your internal coach to blossom to become the parent-teacher.

To enter the world of the great Curriculum you have to realise that true education is about inner knowledge. This therefore means that you are educating your child to awaken their genius. Genius is an experience of oneness. This observation should lead you to the logical conclusion that their exists a oneness; that to awaken your child is an act of liberation. This act must spill out to those around you, to your extended family, to your community.

You should give your child assignments that make them realise this unity with others and the world.

In this book I have tried to show the parent-teacher that all the events in your child's life (and your life) are really calling out the genius in your child. Your role is to facilitate this, to provide a structure for this to happen.

All the steps of the programme have been related to your home and your community. As a parent-teacher it is important that you establish a role between you and your child's school. Over the seventeen years since I've been running Ebony Education I've noticed that most parents feel intimidated by their child's school. There exists an unhealthy relationship between the two. The reasons are partly to do with high exclusion rates, underachievement of African-Caribbean children, the increase in the incidence of bullying, the uncreativity of the National Curriculum, institutional racism, the middle-classness of the teaching profession, the lack of trained parent-teachers etc.

If you the parent-teacher have got this far in this book then you are well on your way to being an effective parent-teacher. It is now time for you to engage with your child's school in a positive manner. Most parents simply turn up at parents evening and listen to the teacher outline their child's progress or lack of progress. This current state of affairs does not lead to the parent being proactive. However, with you having gone through this book, you will now be able to take a number of actions that will help establish a positive partnership, or even establish partnerships with other parents who wish to unlock the genius of their children. Some of these further strategies are listed below:

Family Learning - The Family Study Group

Of course this whole book has been about family learning, but in this section we will focus on the benefits of the family study group. The family study group is when the members of a family (and this can include the extended family) come together at regular intervals and dedicate a certain time to an agreed topic which is to be studied.

It might be an idea to have the topic for your study group meetings on a non-academic subject, and to have it on something that would directly benefit and enrich the family. The topic for the study group might be on starting a family business, or a big holiday trip, or a social issue.

How to set up a Family Study Group

- The aims of the study group should be written down.
- Set clear targets for the group.
- The time, place and date of the study group meetings should be agreed.
- The topic should be of relevance to all and of great interest.
- Games, music and quizzes should be included in the study programme.
- Mind Maps and other study and learning aids should be used.
- All members should take a lead role and gather research material that might include newspaper articles, library books, magazines, tapes.
- Use different learning styles in the learning activity.

In Tony Buzan's book, *Make the Most of Your Mind*, he outlines some of the benefits of the family study group which include:
- A vast increase in the study speed and effectiveness of learning.
- An increase in the family's ability to comprehend any new topic.
- An increase in the family members recall ability.
- Improved Mind Mapping and note-taking skills.
- Strengthened family bonds.
- Improved learning skills and wider interest in a range of subjects.

Possible Structure of a Family Study Group Session (2 hour duration)		
Time	Activity	Outcome
15 mins	• Brain Gym • Yoga (sun salute) • One member tells a joke if appropriate.	Give greater oxygen to brain and neural alertness.
10 mins	Outline sessions aims and recap on last session	Share aims
25 mins	• Share research. • Check member's comprehension to/of task.	Increase information access of all members
25 mins	• Develop mind map • Further develop learning strategy	Increase in knowledge on topic. Improved learning strategies.
10 Mins	Summary outline of session.	Enhanced and shared knowledge on topic studied.

E-Learning and Your Home

Now that your home is equipped with the basics of running your own study group, it is time for you to realise the potential of e-learning.

What is e-learning?

E-learning is when someone uses information and communication technology (ICT) to learn. This ICT might be the internet, interactive games, someone taking an online test, a multimedia presentation etc. By 2010, ICT will become the new basic skill alongside literacy and numeracy.

E-Learning has been made possible by the availability of the internet; improvements in the capability of ICT and its low cost, and the increased use of ICT in subject teaching in schools.

Why is e-learning important?

E-Learning is important because:
▪ It breaks down barriers to learning
▪ It creates learning opportunities
▪ It makes learning environments accessible
▪ It can help stop intergenerational illiteracy as research has found that adults

are twice as likely to participate in learning if they have access to the internet
- Creates employment opportunities like working from home
- Makes information and advice services more accessible
- Improves digital image literacy

From a teaching point of view e-learning offers many opportunities and you can use it to blend in with more traditional teaching. E-Learning helps to improve the quality of teaching by:
- Offering individualising learning packages to learners both young and old
- Can offer personalised learning support
- Link disadvantaged learners to other learners to create collaborative learning experiences
- Allows for more creative and innovative learning, as the teacher and student can create multiple learning experiences
- Allows for flexible learning as the student can study at home, in school, in the library and have access to learning resources anywhere in the world
- Improve learning opportunities for disabled learners
- Suits a variety of learning styles
- Appealing to young people who relate to modern media

For the homeschoolers (children who do not go to school and are educated at home), e-learning is a fantastic opportunity to link up with other home-schoolers and share good practice; offer mutual support and undertake joint projects.

E-Learning is still new and the parent-teacher will have to keep abreast of the new teaching methods and approaches to learning that this new technology offers.

As part of your home education you should establish an e-learning home support resource. You will need to identify the following websites, which once obtained, should prove to be invaluable for at least one academic term.

Website Function	Website Address
For information and advice in education matters	
Online lessons in mathematics, English and Science	
Cultural Website for your cultural group or cultural group which you would like to experience	
Your child's school website	
Children's news/entertainment website	

However, whilst computer technology can give you and your child access to a wide range of educational resources, you should remember that you can learn from nature, by observing a plant grow, or a nature walk, or establishing a project in the garden, or a visit to a local ecology project. The following short story is about a woman who set about establishing such a project, aimed at the education of girls.

Ms Lavene Loves Uncle Joe

People said that it was the greatest love story the little island of Carriacou had ever seen. They said it was a wonderful romance between Ms Lavene, a young woman from a poor family, who, when she was eleven won a scholarship to go to Grenada to study but her parents made her turn it down because they couldn't afford it. Apparently, that's how things were back in 1931. They said she cried for weeks, burying her head in her pillow and tangled plaits. Yes, her school teachers said she was the brightest girl ever to have come out of Mount Pleasant School. They even said she could have been a doctor for she always wanted to know about medicine; how to cure the sick and the poor, and she wanted to know the secrets of the Universe. In some respects Uncle Joe was similar, though his great quest for learning was satisfied when he left the island, went to Trinidad in a fisherman's boat and later got a job on a big ship that took him around the world. He had always wanted to be a great poet, and the travel now gave him a million and one things to write his poetry about. He was a big, muscular, rich-brown man, with a deep chuckle in his voice and he wore a thick belt around his waist. Ms Lavene was a very slim black woman who never recovered from her lost opportunity and always sought to venture beyond the tiny shores of Carriacou. When she met Uncle Joe, one April when he was on leave, she suddenly discovered the world that she had longed for in his stories and songs which he embellished with a quatro he played. Six months after they met they were married under the Sapodilla tree, and half the people from this tiny island came to wish them well and listen to Uncle Joe read her his poetry that made her blush.

For five years they remained happily married. Their love produced a little girl child who bore all the traits of Ms Lavene, and she too started to attend Mount Pleasant Elementary School. One day, when Uncle Joe was back on the island having gone to South America where he wrote poems about mermaids, Ms Lavene found him under the Sapodilla tree where he continued to write his poetry, believing that he had at last written his greatest poem ever. But Ms Lavene was irritated, she wanted him to do extra work in town, to raise a little money so that their daughter could go to the big school on mainland Grenada and get the education she never had.

"Woman," he said vexed. "You can't see me writing me poetry."

"Joe, everyday you writing poetry, and every poem you write soun' de same." At this Uncle Joe got cross. "Woman, sit down and listen to me new.."

"Me don't 'ave time to.."

"Woman sit down and listen." Reluctantly, she sat down under the tree as he cleared his throat and began to read. When he finished he said:

"So what you t'ink?" She mused for a while.

"It okay, but it lack balance. It unbalance." Apparently, according to my father, Uncle Joe got up in a rage and shouted. "Balance? Wha' you know 'bout balance?" Ms Lavene, wanting to stand her ground and speak the truth, walked out of the shadow of the tree and said: " It lack harmony and metaphor. Uncle Joe, who had never had anyone from the island challenge his poetry, well not to his face, was now brown-red with fury. " 'armony and mata what! Woman, never speak bout me poetry again!"

From that day onwards their marriage became strained. He stopped writing her letters when he went away, he stopped reading her his poetry when he returned and he would argue with Ms Lavene, regarding the correct education for their daughter. Anyway, one day Uncle Joe went to work on a ship, but this time he didn't come back. Ms Lavene, would stand under the Sapodilla tree and look out into the blue sea, but as the months went by she could hardly see for the tears that half blinded her to the reality that Uncle Joe had left her and the child.

Three miserable years passed. We never heard much from Ms Lavene, until one winter evening, the front door bell rang. My mother, who had been in the back room pressing hair, came and opened the door. And there, with a hat that made her even more ridiculous because of the snow was Ms Lavene and an old suitcase. Ms Lavene had come to England. All I can remember was everyone fussing round this Caribbean woman, and a big cup of Ovaltine being brought for her, as she warmed herself by the coal fire that my father stoked hurriedly.

"How Joe can leave me. Me heart break. Help me find Joe na!" The very next day, Dad put on his hat and coat, kissed mum on the cheek and headed up to Liverpool where he heard Uncle Joe was on leave from his ship. Some five hours later, Dad stood with a crumpled up piece of paper outside a tall run down house in a back street where dogs and children played. Dad banged on the door. No one answered. He banged again, and this time a tall, dark haired woman opened the door, blowing smoke in Dad's face, as she then turned in her dressing gown and said, "Joe, you have a visitor." She then went into the other room, apparently without even giving Dad another glance. The two men hugged warmly, before cracking open a bottle of rum, raising their glass and saying, "For all those who gone before us." When they settled down, Dad told Uncle Joe that he couldn't just walk out on his family over a poem. "But she tell me me poem don't 'ave balance. Den she start talk 'bout meta-somet'ing." According to my Dad he didn't say anything much after that. Just looked into the wisdom of his glass of rum and left Uncle Joe with these words. "You better reach back to Carriacou."

Another year or so passed. By this time Ms Lavene had returned to the small island, where, under the Sapodilla tree she sat and read all of Uncle Joe's books on poetry, history and philosophy. It was as if she was finally getting the education that she had missed when her family decided against her taking up the offer of a scholarship. After she read all of his books she would carry her grandmother's *One Drum* down to the Sapodilla tree and beat a rhythm of perfect harmony. Apparently, this went on for some nine years, by which time Ms Lavene's daughter was eleven, and she to had won a scholarship to go to the mainland and study at the senior school. But this time, Ms Lavene, who now wore all white and jewellery of cowrie shells, told her daughter no. Me will give you de education you need. Me don't wan' your heart break like mine. From that day onwards, every evening, Ms Lavene would sit under the tree and talk, and she played the *One Drum*. Soon, other women got to hear about the Talk of *One Drum,* and they brought their daughters to listen, and before long a great gathering assembled each night. According to my mother, Ms Lavene, inspired by the Maroon women who started *One Drum*, organised the education of girls, and told them about the harmonic systems on the earth that they had been put on the earth to realise and maintain. One of her most recorded lectures in the folklore of the islanders was entitled, the Circle of Womanhood.
That night, under the biggest moon people had ever seen, Ms Lavene made all the girls and women sit in a big circle round the Sapodilla tree, whilst one of them played *One Drum*, as she walked about the circle, at first casting spells in Igbo, then finally starting her talk.

"De education of girl child is 'bout de knowledge of harmonic systems dat make de world. We sit in circle because it symbolise de equal love and respect we must 'ave for one another. De whole universe did start from circle, and from circle everyt'ing reach, and de circle produce harmonic sound, and de sound 'ave power, but you can only understand and access dis power, when you make harmony in your ownself. Everyt'ing balanced. Dere is woman principle and man principle that lie behind everyt'ing on de earth. It our job to make sure dat dese principles are balanced. We must organise de education of girl child and boy child so dem know to balance tings. Dem should study science, literature, history, language, mathematics and even poetry. But dem must know how everyt'ing connect."

Apparently, Uncle Joe was there looking on. He was almost unrecognisable. In London and Paris, together with the bohemian actress that he had fallen in love with because she said his poetry was delightful, he had known fame. He read at avant garde literary functions, until the actress who had now fallen in love with a younger man, told Uncle Joe that his poetry lacked harmony. So, according to my parents, there he was with a thick beard, blood-shot eyes, and tattered clothes. The following evening he waited for Ms Lavene under the tree. "Lavene," he said with tears in his eyes. "It me, Joe. You was right. My poetry lack understanding, it lack understanding of you, you as a woman. Take me back Lavene. Me will love you wid all me heart." At first Ms Lavene was going to say no, but something stopped her. She turned to the man that she once loved so much and said. "If you can learn to play *One Drum* in perfect harmony, me will take you back." So, for months, and some said even years, Uncle Joe sat under the Sapodilla tree and practiced playing *One Drum,* listening to his own rhythm, and the rhythm of the universe, until one day he finally mastered it.

He and Ms Lavene lived until their nineties to see their daughter become a teacher. My mum would always tell me that I'm from this tradition, that whenever I set up a new education project I must remember this story, for education is ultimately the understanding of the harmony of the universe and self. In designing a curriculum, what must be central is the understanding of the feminine and masculine principles, the duality that underlies the world, and the harmonic systems that manifest as world events and things. Ms Lavene challenged the patriarchy of the islanders; she instituted non-institutional education, she introduced an economic system of barter that helped the poor; her students would watch the opening of a healing flower and she would watch the opening of their minds. And she showed that education is about womanhood, and womanhood is a spiritual practice. Ms Lavene, one might say, is the inspiration behind this book. It is the women like her, who secretly educated other women and men during the times of slavery, that kept an unacknowledged genius alive.

The most effective empowerment of girls and young women is education. This was what Ms Lavene was about. An educated girl or young woman will improve their health care and those of their family; lower infant mortality, be less vulnerable to child labour and sexual abuse, raise the economic growth of the community and in certain parts of the world help stop the spread of AIDS. Three-quarters of the one billion people in the world who cannot read or write are girls and women. You may live in a part of the world where you think these issues are not such a pressing concern, but they are. The abuse against your fellow human beings is your concern, and your child's concern. Educate your child about these issues as Ms Lavene did.

So her legacy to me and to you is this Learning Tree, this book. Each time I write I sit under Ms Lavene's Sapodilla Tree. Our Learning Tree must be understood both literally and metaphorically. It takes energy from the sun and gives life to the world. It is always giving; it gives more than it receives. It gives me the blessing of the meditative shade in which I write. It brings those with wisdom to me and empowers and humbles my work. It gives nutrients to the soil, and takes a story from the ancestors and makes it a gift to the next generation. Our Tree is always in harmony. It was, and perhaps still is Ms Lavene's temple. Is it ours? Yes? Well then, may our Tree take root.

Conduct basic research into:
- E-learning for children.
- Family literacy/learning.
- The education of girls and young women.

A Poetical Gift to You From the Tree

Ms Lavene's Song

Understand me if I scold your lazy gaze;
I secret astrologer of your solar energy.

Understand me my creation of noise,
As I watch your galaxy at play.

Understand my lonely parenthood,
My quarrels that weed your tangled life.

Understand my knowledge of heavens cosmology;
It is so you will be the eternal star.

The Genius Child: citizenship and world issues

Key words/themes: peace, relaxation

Aims:
- To increase the awareness of the parent-teacher to the ultimate goal of education which is peace.

African Proverb
Those at peace work for it
                Zambia

Your lifestyle of peace and relaxation is the constant lesson to the child. They are no longer seeing you tense, angry or fearful. This emotional stability is their great lesson.

Peace and the Curriculum of Genius

Imagine that you have been told about the greatest school in the world where the children are getting top grades, and so you decide to send your child there. When you are shown into the class it is completely empty. There are no chairs, no desks, no books, no pictures and you are told that there isn't even a syllabus or curriculum. For some strange reason you decide to leave your child there. Three thirty arrives and you pick your child up. When you enter the classroom your child is content and totally at peace. You then notice that this peacefulness has become the foundation upon which their growing genius is based, for they have no fears; they have no negative thoughts telling them they can't achieve, or memories of failure, or a teacher having low expectation, because they are at peace with this curriculum of genius.

This is what this educational programme is; the curriculum of genius and you now must make your home/community the classroom, the school that contains everything to unlock the genius of your child.

Learning Models in Nature

Use nature to inspire you and to extract models from. A model used to look at the cognitive style in numeracy is the 'grasshopper' versus the 'inchworm'. The approach taken by the inchworm to problem solving is a step by step approach, whereas the grasshopper makes intuitive leaps, and deals with problems using a variety of strategies. This model helps in the understanding of the cognitive styles of different learners, and how the two hemispheres of the brain process information. The Nigerian scientist, Philip Emeagwali, who won the Gordon Bell Prize, developed his programming formulae (3.1 billion processes per second) by getting the idea from watching bees build their honeycombs. Apparently no other creature works more efficiently than a community of bees building a honey comb.

Again we see that quiet observation and an appreciation of nature can educate the observer, enrich the learning experience and provide scientific models.

The Parent-Teacher Letter

A Mother's Letter to the Headteacher

Dear Ms Maudsley,

Now dat tear stop drop from me eye, me just wan' say few words "bout me son exclusion. Darren is aware what him do was wrong; him apology in him silence, and it there when him stare out window and look pon our apple tree. Is God dat give him to me; so me can't abandon him like you do. You call it permanent exclusion. It mean abandon same way. No, when a mother suckle dem child, wipe sleep from dem eye, watch dem foot start walk when dem likkle, dem can't abandon dem child. From what Darren say him hit de teacher, cause de man did mock de plaits Darren keep in him head; tell Darren off for de way him walk, and even say Darren don't sing properly in assembly. De teacher is suppose to be a teacher, not a policeman. For now, me and me husband gone keep Darren home, before we go look another school. We trying we best to educate him with de few book we have pon we shelf.

We as parent blame ourself. We believed you. Believed your school reports. Believed that him underachieve; believe what you say "bout how him forget spelling pattern, grammar, and number business. Me know dat you 'ave children too. Believed that we as woman could relate. Dat we 'ave ting in common. Yes, dere differences. You keep your head in perm, me have locks. You wear tweed skirt me wear jeans. You eat roast beef, and potato wid white sauce, but me eat rice and peas and chicken. You read T.S. Eliot, I read Palms. You go on holiday to Devon, I go back-a-yard. But we woman still. Or so me did tink until you and your teachers turn on me son. Aren't we in de same world. Don't we breathe de same air, live under de same sky? You excluded Darren from hope, from your trust. But you excluded your ownself from your own womanhood. Woman was put pon dis earth to heal. Not mash-up dreams of likkle black child.

We believed you. We did even give him some licks, until one day, Darren invite him friend over for tea. A likkle white boy who nose keep run. Him and Darren is good friend from dem small dem play for hours, until it home time and de child leave. But him friend forget him reading book dat de teacher write comments in. When we open de book we find de teacher write plenty words of encouragement; praise de child, suggest ways to boost him reading, say how hard him trying. How come de teacher never say dat bout Darren. Him was only five. We as a family trusted your school. Come to de fund raising event; come to silly likkle boot fair, and Christmas carol dat almost make we sleep, and all de time you had no ambition for my child. Never did listen to him hearts dream, him soul enquiring 'bout de world, and him shyness daring to move aside so him big-up him likkle self. You ambush him dreams. We as a family was naive. We believed that a school is a school. But it not! It full of politics. It full of likkle eliteness; middle class people getting dem child through. It full of teacher like Darren teacher, testing, and selecting; deciding who will have what type of education. Your curriculum ambush him future. We wanted a curriculum to unlock him soul; not just package information.

De last meeting that we did keep wid you, you sit infront of us in your green trouser suit. You explain what exclusion mean; talk like you telling us 'bout de weather. Is me son you ah deal wid! We could hardly speak. Him get exclude. It was dat simple to you. We leave your office, our head mad wid anger, and we in daze. We walk in silence. Two minute later I remember me scarf me leave, so I return, and when me reach back you having party in your office; you celebrating good school results; and everyone was drinking tea, eating biscuits. Every'ing was as it should be in your world. And you did even have on your Friend of de Earth badge. How come your not my friend? How come your not Darren friend? How come your not my family friend?

You see, you excluded Darren from de moment him start school. You exclude him from encouragement, from ambition, from hope. So him rebell. He been rebelling since him four. I noticed it once, but I didn't understand it. De first day him start school him run; run to de gates and look in, sensing dat him was gone learn everyt'ing in de world. But as time go on; as autumn get more chill, him run stop, and him head drop; soon him start to say dat him don't wan' go school. I ask him why, but him wouldn't say. At dat age him can't speak what deep inside of him. And you know what, as him get big him join gang. This de same gang dat you write to me 'bout. You say it bad company and I start panic. But now, I understand. Now me realise dat him move with gang because it give him de education to survive in de wicked school system. It give him some respect, some self-esteem, and some hope. You see, everyone have gang. You have your gang. Your Special Education needs teacher, your educational psychiatrist, your deputy Head, your social workers. Dem is all your gang, and dem vandalise Darren! De Darren you have report on, and de Darren that you exclude don't really exist. You and your gang created him to make your gang get big salary. Darren is a beautiful child. Him quiet and proud like him father, and is dis proudness dat make him not stand for insult from your teacher. Your gang lay a trap for him, but now me will teach him strategy.

Each night, though I tired wid work dat society consign to us women, I does hug meself up and sit out on de patio and just look at Moon; watch her good wid she quiet wisdom, and wait for her to say, Yvonne, just keep strong; drink some bush, take some aloe vera; eat some gunga pea soup, and sprinkle some joy in it too. And one night she tell me; teach your child yourself. Well doubt, make me jump out of me chair and cuss some bad words at Moon, but she stay de same way. She wait for cloud to pass, smile and just say: "Wasn't it you who did born first pon this earth? Wasn't it you who did grow crop pon de Nile banks? Wasn't it you who did suckle Imhotep, and Nefartari, and Malcolm and Martin? And for de first time my heart start sing; sing to de world announcing my child's genius. I want to run and celebrate; tell everyone dat me is gone be me son teacher. Following day we take Darren to museum, where all our history covered in cobweb. First, him shake him head, say him don't wan' go, but we coax him, and after awhile him foot skip down de steps. When we reach, we look at ancient dis and ancient dat; never realising dat all de museums is bout we history; 'bout we magic, and architecture, and science. Akan,

Bantu, Youruba and ting. We history was rich, and den the museum show video of Tutankhamun; a likkle boy just few years bigger than Darren. Him did rule de most powerful nation on earth. Darren get excited and puzzle, though him did try and hide it. When we reach home, Darren drop him jacket pon de floor in de hall, run to de computer and go on internet. Him search for everyt'ing bout dis likkle black boy king; couldn't understand how black child can have power, can sit pon throne like him belong there. I realise then that this is what me must teach him; teach him bout power; bout who have money power, who have economic power, bout who have media power, and perhaps most of all, who have God's power. Perhaps, this is my job; perhaps me was wrong for even dream dat you can reach in to him heart and teach him dese tings. Yes, one day my son will sit pon him throne, and him will hold staff and sceptre, and him will command de souls of people who seek an education dat ultimately lead dem to God.

Ms Maudsley, we wish you well. We as a family are not bitter. We disappointed. It time you really look into de hearts of de children you supposed to educate. Look into dem soul. One day their love will be your salvation. Me write dis letter under our apple tree, under our Learning Tree me should say; and from Darren exclusion, now everyt'ing fill wid possibility. Darren get up dis morning and for de first time I see him fascinated 'bout de world. He not hearing condemnation; he not feeling like him can't learn. Now, him dreaming bout him own throne; de throne of genius dat we preparing for him.

Yours sincerely,

Mother of Genius Child

Your Child's Citizenship and World Issues

So now that we have come to the end, you, the parent-teacher are ready start on a new journey to discover your child's and your own genius through soulful enquiry, research and action. But this programme is more than simply just supporting your child, for I never started out with such selfish and localised goals; it is about children, and other potential parent-teachers, and their communities. One billion people in the world do not go to school and cannot read or write. What can individuals do? Yes, support our children but the greatest education that you can give your child, is for them to see you attempting to help others, and doing this with joy. The danger of the present education system is that it places us in an illusion. The illusion is that science and technology is progressing society, that things are getting better, that this science and technology will defeat the great issues of today (and tomorrow); 'Third World debt', environmental issues, racism, war and world illiteracy. In the West we can easily pursue a lifestyle that escapes all of this, but can we? One day, some day something will happen and we, like the news services, will label it an unexpected disaster. It will only be unexpected because we chose to live in an illusion.

At present the world of education is full of slick sounding buzz words and schemes; global economy, knowledge economy, transferable skills, individual education/learning plans, vocation, inclusiveness, basic skills etc. But those who have traditionally underachieved, still underachieve. Education is a multi billion industry. To many, the school is a market, where children have to be prepared for industry, whether this preparation is in the interest of the child or not, or even if economic planning that has prompted government policy is accurate or not.

To the West, Globalisation is the innocent pursuit of global markets. To those in the so called Third World it means ecological devastation and selfish economic policies that results in world poverty. In *Hidden Connections*, Fritjof Capra outlines how in natural ecosystems no group is excluded from the network of the whole, but Globalisation works against this model of a natural system, as it excludes people from its benefits. Your child is the *Future Child*. They will inherit a world of patented crops, genetically engineered food, racism, the exploitation of girls and women; international crime, the movement of mass refugees and political instability. How will the *Future Child* make sense of this? This global crisis calls for a new education system. This education system can only come about as a global grassroots movement. It will be led by the most concerned; the parents and the children.

This book is a call for the parent-teacher to take positive action and give the opportunity to all to have a meaningful and safe opportunity to education. It is also an attempt to present a unified curriculum that is aimed at making a better human in a sustainable society.

A Poetical Gift From the Tree to You

The Education of the Dumb Child

It started in the corner of the world of the dumb child,
Not understanding the geometry of school,

He now wore the uniform of shame,
After September's optimism flew away.
It was on Old Dreary Hill,
When they climbed through the fog,
Where he burnt their lesson plans,
Cursed his own stammer.

Yes, they took him away
To the sad jail for children,
Where he swore to avenge his illiteracy,
So he could loosen the ropes of his report.

The corner of the world lost the dumb child;
He escaped to the sweet life of easy crime,
Where his curse hid his stammer,
Until an old hunched judge sent him back to the corner.

The cell became the classroom,
Jailers stalked his learning,
The subtle magic of poems rescued his soul,
There, in the stench of the cell
He tamed the violence of the words,
Screamed down the grammar of their ambush.

Then, parole released his poetry.
Now, he makes revolutionary scribbles,
To the children of his footsteps
For the 'dumb' child has unlocked his genius.

Glossary of Educational Terms

The professional world of education is full of terminology that parents can find difficult to understand. Below is a simple glossary of educational terms to help the parent understand the jargon so as not to feel excluded and intimidated by these terms which often appear in end of year reports, reports of educational psychiatrists, literature issued by the educational establishments etc.

ADHD	Attention Deficit Hyperactivity Disorder.
Attainment Targets	What children should knew at different levels (1 - 8).
Autism	A complex neurological disorder that usually appears in the first three years of life. Children and adults who have autism have difficulties with verbal and non-verbal communication.
CATs	Cognitive Abilities Tests. Multiple choice tests that give a measure of a child's capability.
Core Subjects	English, Maths and Science. These subjects are studied by all children.
Curriculum	The subjects and areas taught to children
DfEE	Department for Education and Employment.
Digraph	two letters standing for one sound (phoneme) eg sh.
Dyslexia	A reading and spelling disorder.
Etymology	the study of words
Foundation Stage	The curriculum provided for children 3, 4 and 5.
Homophones	words that sound alike but have different meanings.
INSET	In-Service Education and Training - for practising teachers.
Key Stage	Age-related divisions of the curriculum based on traditional school grouping of children.
NFER	National foundation for Educational Research in England and Wales.

Phonics — an all inclusive term that teaches a reading method based on the sounds of letters.

Phonology — the study of sounds in language.

'real books' — a learning method that encourages the child to read based on natural language ability.

SaTs — Standard Assessment Tests used for the National Crurriculum.

SEN — Special Educational Needs.

Suffix — a syllable added to the end of the word to change the meaning of the word.

Syllable — a unit of sound within a word

Selected Bibliography

Amen, Ra Un Nefer. 1996. *Tree of Life Meditation System*: Kamit Publications.
Apple, Michael. 1995. *Education and Power*. Routledge
Baker, Sidney Macdonald. 2003 *Detoxification and Healing*: Contemporary Books.
Baruti, K. Kafele 1991. A Black Parent's Handbook to Educating Your Children: Baruti Publishing.
Bocchino, Rob 1999. *Emotional Literacy: To be a different kind of smart*. Corwin Press.
Boyd, Hamish 1981. *Introduction to Homoeopathic Medicine*: Beaconsfield Publishers Ltd.
Buzan, Tony. 1977. *Make the Most of Your Mind*. Colt Books Ltd.
Capra, Fritjof. 2002. *The Hidden Connections*, Harper Collins.
Dare, Angela & O'Donovan, Margaret. 2002. *A Practical Guide to Child Nutrition*. Nelson Thornes.
Davenport, G.C. 1994. *An Introduction to Child Development*: Collins.
De Bono, Edward. 1993. *Teach Your Child How to Think*: Penguin
Edwards, Betty. 1992. *Drawing on the Right Side of the Brain*: Harper Collins Publishers
Feldman, William. 2002. *Learning and Attention Disorders*: Constable and Robinson Ltd.
Tynan, Bernadette. 2004. *Your Child Can Think Like a Genius*: Thorsons
Holford, Patrick. 1997. *The Optimum Nutrition Bible*: Piatkus Ltd.
Liebeck, Pamela. 1984. *How Children Learn Mathematics*: Pelican Books Litd.
McGuinness, Diane. 1997. *Why Children Can't Read*: Penguin Books.
McGuinness & McGuinness, Carmen & Geoffrey. 1998. *Reading Reflex*: Penguin.
Montessori, Maria. 1991. *The Advanced Montessori Method - 1*: Clio Press.
Mukerjea, Dilip. 1996. *Superbrain*: Oxford University Press.
Wilson, Amos. 1991. *Awakening the Natural Genius of Black Children*: Afrikan World Infosystems.